HYPER THE GRACE GOSPEL

—— **PAUL ELLIS** ——

KINGSPRESS
Birkenhead, New Zealand

ENDORSEMENTS

Michael Brown has unknowingly paid a great compliment to those of us who teach and write about the gospel of grace. To label us hyper-grace teachers puts us in some exceptional company, such as the Apostle Paul! Paul Ellis has masterfully answered Michael Brown's criticisms and untangled many of the distortions his book represents. For that, I am profoundly grateful. This book is a must read!

— CLARK WHITTEN
　　Pastor, Grace Church, Orlando, FL, and author of *Pure Grace*

I can think of no better person to respond to the accusations against the modern grace message than my friend, Paul Ellis. His defense is filled with exactly what I would expect—respect, wisdom, and an abundance of grace. Those reading his new book, *The Hyper Grace Gospel*, will be pleased to find, not an argumentative treatise, but a love story of redemption and forgiveness that provides hope for the entire world.

— LUCAS MILES
　　President, The Oasis Network For Churches

Paul Ellis' new book exposes the misrepresentations and misunderstandings of many Christians concerning the grace message and grace believers. This book will not only help you to see the flaws of a mixed gospel, it will help you to find your true self. It is the modern day Magna Carta of Christianity.

— SIMON YAP WEI TOONG
　　Teacher, The Grace Place Kuala Lumpur, blogger at His Grace is Enough

Paul Ellis' new book *The Hyper-Grace Gospel*, is a brilliant and insightful response to Dr Brown's objections, as well as the many other myths and misunderstandings that some have about the message of grace. I highly recommend it.

— ED ELLIOTT
　　President, Word of Life World Outreach

I have never read anything by Paul Ellis that I didn't love. His laser-sharp focus on Jesus, his commitment to the authority of Scripture, and his gracious demeanor go a long way in clearing the air with the grace and truth of our Savior. *The Hyper-Grace Gospel* is no exception. It should be read by anyone who wants to understand this current reformation and return to the too-good-be-true message of salvation and life in Christ!

— JEREMY WHITE
　　Pastor, Valley Church, Vacaville, CA, and author of *The Gospel Uncut*

All I can say about this book is that I wanted to write a book in response to Michael Brown's book and have no need to do so anymore. This is a more than a sufficient, answer to the logic followed by Dr. Brown. It is a must read.

— BERTIE BRITS
　　Pastor, Dynamic Love Ministries, South Africa

In his new book Paul Ellis clarifies the central tenets of the gospel message while answering its critics with clarity and grace. Truly the gospel is the liberating good news of a God who loves us beyond what we can imagine. That message is worth defending and Paul does so eloquently. This book may well become a handbook for all who preach God's glorious grace.

— TONY IDE
Pastor, Freedom Life Church, Perth, Australia

As a preacher who has been labeled "hyper-grace," I found myself with a grin from ear to ear as I read this book. People have always twisted the message of grace into a false message that they could attack. It's refreshing to see someone dealing with these issues in the same manner as the Apostle Paul. Bypassing straw-man arguments, Paul Ellis writes concisely, yet comprehensively, all the while preaching the truth in grace and love. It's this skill that makes him one of my favorite authors.

— PHIL DRYSDALE
PhilDrysdale.com, author of *You Do Not Have a Sinful Nature*

Grace that is misunderstood, is grace that is not received. In this book, Paul Ellis brings amazing clarity and understanding to grace, which is the very essence of the gospel. I highly recommend *The Hyper-Grace Gospel*.

— CHRIS BARHORST
Pastor, True Life Church, Greenville, OH

Paul Ellis may have written this as a response to Dr. Brown's book but the result is an excellent picture of the importance of having a sure foundation in the true love and grace of God. This is a great book to give to anyone to show them the contrast between religious-based and grace-based Christianity.

— TED NELSON
Pastor, The Grace Station, Wausau, WI

The message of grace has drawn its fair share of judgment. While confronting issues and answering critics in our own corners of the globe, many of us shake our heads in frustration at the same old arguments rising up in new places. In Paul Ellis' work, we have found a voice that says, in a concise and all-encompassing way, what many of us have said. Now that someone wrote it down, we can all continue the business of making Jesus look good.

— PAUL WHITE
Pastor, Midland Church, Poplar Bluff, author *Revelation to Transformation*

Whilst I am not generally fond of dialogue which draws attention to doctrinal differences and disagreements amongst Christians, many of the New Testament epistles exist only because of this very thing. And we are all the better for it. I commend both Michael Brown and Paul Ellis for their courage and convictions, and for encouraging us to engage with such a worthy subject matter. Amazing grace, how sweet the sound!

— CHAD M. MANSBRIDGE
Pastor, Bayside Int. Church, Australia, and author of *He Qualifies You*

I believe Dr. Michael Brown has a passion to protect the gospel and for that I commend and respect him. However, in my opinion, his understanding of the gospel is not quite rightly divided between the new and old covenants. It has some misinterpretations that clearly contradict new covenant doctrine. His views unfortunately put him at odds with many great preachers of today who also love the Word of God and are passionate about keeping the gospel pure. I'm glad Paul Ellis has written a response to Dr. Michael Brown's book. Paul's response is fair, well written, gracious, and respectful. It's not a fight or an argument but a straightforward response to a view that undermines the new covenant, our faith, the goodness of God, the way we relate to God, and what motivates us to live for Jesus.

— RYAN RUFUS
Pastor, City Church Int., Hong Kong, and author of *After the Revolution*

In Jesus you're forgiven, sanctified, made holy and eternally righteousness, yet Dr. Brown says Jesus isn't enough. Now he wouldn't come right out and say such a thing but Dr. Ellis pinpoints with laser sharp accuracy where Dr. Brown still depends on human effort to complete the work Jesus began. Paul Ellis' response to Dr. Brown is one of respect and brotherly love. It's refreshing to see mature communication on such a hotly debated issue. Paul's explanation of grace and sanctification brings a degree of clarity often missed in Christianity today. To quote Dr. Ellis, "The hyper-grace gospel is easy to recognize for it is nothing more than boasting about Jesus."

— CLINT BYARS
Pastor, Forward Church, Atlanta, GA, and author of *Good God*

How saved are we? In Paul Ellis' doubt-erasing new book, we are expertly guided into the truth that our salvation consists wholly in the historic biblical doctrine of pure grace, empowered by the message of unfailingly good news, and is accomplished through the singularly glorious work of Jesus Christ. Marvelous truth!

— CHUCK CRISCO
Author of *Extraordinary Gospel: Experiencing the Goodness of God*

The Hyper-Grace Gospel: A Response to Michael Brown and Those Opposed to the Modern Grace Message

ISBN: 978–1–927230–33–6
Copyright © 2014 by Paul Ellis

Published by KingsPress, Birkenhead, New Zealand. This title is also available as a paperback and an ebook. Visit www.KingsPress.org for information.

Version: 1.2 (April 2015)

Dedication: This is for everyone who dares to preach the hyper-grace gospel!

Contents

Introduction

What is the one thing that sets Christianity apart from every other religion in the world? It is not turning from sin, prayer, confession, or moral living, for all these practices can be found, in one form or another, in other religions. The one thing that makes the Christian faith unique is grace.

Grace is God's divine favor and loving-kindness toward you. Grace is God blessing you with Himself for no other reason than it pleases Him to do so. Need proof? Look to the cross where "Christ died for the ungodly" (Rom. 5:6). Christ did not die for the good and the great and those on the top of the ladder. He died for the weak and the lost and the poor and the needy.

Christ gave His life for those who need life. To those honest enough to say, "Help! I don't have it all together," God responds, "I am your very great Helper." That's grace.

Grace is not a doctrine but a Person and His name is Jesus. Grace is not one of God's blessings but all of them wrapped up together in Christ.

Grace is the Gift of all gifts from the Giver of all givers.

I'm addicted to grace like I'm addicted to oxygen. I can honestly say I would rather not live if I can't have it and I would probably be dead without it. It is God's amazing grace that has brought me safe thus far and His grace will lead me home.

I am in the business of telling people the good news of God's grace. I write so that you may know that God loves you like a Father. No matter what you've done or how bad you've been, your heavenly Father holds nothing against you. He longs to hug you and kiss you and take care of you and be with you forever.

The good news that brings great joy is that God is not against us but He is for us and with us and through Christ He is *in us.*

The grace of God is infinitely better than the dead religions of earth. Religion says you have to get cleaned up before you can come to God but grace declares, "Come as you are!" Religion says you need to do this and that but grace insists Jesus has done it all. Religion says you have to keep the rules and make sacrifices but grace proclaims Christ has kept all the rules on your behalf and His sacrifice has no sequel.

1

The power of love

Recently, a man told me how he and his wife lost three babies during pregnancy. Then they lost the ability to have any children. At that time they were a part of a church that preached performance-based Christianity. The message they heard was, "Do well and God will bless you." It was a false promise. The man and his wife had done well but they weren't blessed. Instead, they were condemned, ridiculed, and worn out.

Then the man heard Jesus speaking grace over him and everything changed. Captivated by the goodness of their Father, the couple was set free from the unholy demands of religion. Where previously they had been striving to secure the blessings of God, the man could now say, "My wife and I are at rest in Jesus." The supernatural grace of God healed them and now they have three healthy boys. They have become living testimonies of the healing power of their Father's love.

I hear stories like this all the time. I know people who would have died, marriages that would have ended, and families that would have been destroyed except the grace of a good God inter-vened and brought heaven to earth.

The gospel of grace declares that God loves you with a love you cannot measure. To quote Philip Yancey, "Grace means there is nothing I can do to make God love me more, and nothing I can do to make God love me less."[1]

God does not love you because you are good or decent or because you wear a suit on Sundays. He loves you because He is your Father. The reason you exist is because God had a dream and wrapped it up in you. You are your Daddy's dream come true.

D.L. Moody once said, "If you ask me why God should love us, I cannot tell. I suppose it is because He is a true Father."[2]

And what a good Father He is! We rejected Him, but He did not reject us. We ran and hid, but He came and found us. He does not treat us as our sins deserve (Ps. 103:10).

Contrary to what you may have heard, God is not frowning at you. He is smiling at you with infinite delight. This may be news to you but I hope you will agree that it is *good* news. Indeed, it is the "the good, glad, merry news" that seventeenth-century preachers said "makes a man fairly leap for joy!"[3]

The apostle Paul referred to the gospel as the "glad-message of ... the happy God" (1 Tim. 1:11, Rotherham's Emphasized Bible). The gospel declares that God is happy and through Christ He has given you everything you need for life and wholeness.

A friend of mine wrote on my Facebook page: "Knowing how loved I am makes me want to dance for a million years!" This is a normal reaction to the gospel of grace. When you see how good your Father is and how much He cares for you, it makes you want to shout and leap and attempt great things.

Those who are secure in their Father's love stride the earth with a supernatural confidence. They release the fragrance of Jesus wherever they go. They shine in dark places, bring freedom to captives, and release the oppressed. In the name of their Father they give grace to the hurting and life to the dead.

And this is why it saddens me to find some who are opposed to the glad-happy message of God's amazing grace.

The backlash against the grace message

In the past few months, there has been an aggressive backlash against the gospel of grace. This backlash has been seen in the Christian media, the blogosphere, and in the publication of books by respected Bible teachers. I have come across articles with titles like "Confronting the error of hyper-grace," "The deception of hyper-grace," and the oddly-titled, "What's wrong with grace?"

The authors of these articles typically describe the gospel of grace as a "dangerous teaching," a "false message," and "a hyped-up, watered-down, seeker-friendly gospel." Those who preach it are branded "false prophets," "antichrists," and "pied pipers" leading people to hell.

What do these critics have against the gospel of grace? Their criticisms are numerous. The grace message is soft on sin. It's opposed to the law. It's a prosperity gospel. It's unbalanced. It's extreme. It's a fad.

Some of these criticisms reflect abiding misperceptions ("grace promotes licentiousness"). Others are just wrong ("grace is universalism in disguise"). Some of the criticisms are slanderous ("grace preachers are closet sinners"), while others are risible ("this message was responsible for the rise of Adolph Hitler and the runaway Democratic party").

Presented with these sorts of claims, it is tempting to dismiss the opponents of the grace message as ill informed and reactionary. But not all of them are.

In January 2014, Dr. Michael L. Brown released a book entitled *Hyper-Grace: Exposing the Dangers of the Modern Grace Message*. In his book, Dr. Brown seeks to correct "some serious distortions and errors" that are being preached as part of what he calls "the modern grace message." Dr. Brown portrays hyper-grace preachers as being opposed to repentance and the confession of sins, and he claims we think the words of Jesus have no relevance for us today. Is this true? Do hyper-grace preachers actually think this way?

Since I am one of the hyper-grace preachers identified by Dr. Brown, I thought it might be helpful to respond to these accusations. As we will see, a number of them are based on misperceptions or they misrepresent what we are actually saying. Yet other accusations are spot on. On several occasions reading his book I said to myself, "Guilty as charged," and I did so with a grace-addict's grin.

I said I was one of the hyper-grace preachers. Who are the others preaching this "distorted and dangerous" message of grace?

In chapter 1 of his book, Dr. Brown identifies six hyper-grace preachers: Joseph Prince, Clark Whitten, Steve McVey, Andrew Farley, Rob Rufus, and me. I am honored to be included in such a group. In his book Dr. Brown also cites the sermons and writings of Andrew Wommack, Andre van der Merwe, Benjamin Dunn, Chuck Crisco, John Crowder, Mick Mooney, Andre Rabe, and Ryan Rufus. In addition, Dr. Brown further identifies in relatively few places; Rob Bell, Colin Dye, Francois du Toit, John Sheasby, Sam Storms, Jeff Turner, Tony Ide, Michael Reyes, and Simon Yap. I am familiar with the work of most of these men and count several of them as my friends.

One could argue that Dr. Brown has missed quite a few influential grace preachers. On my blog, Escape to Reality, I have a book review page where you will find more than 50 grace-based books. Many of these seemed to have been missed by Dr. Brown. Since my list is not comprehensive and excludes preachers who don't write books, then Dr. Brown's smaller list can be said to be far from exhaustive. But that may not be a problem if those he cites are representative of the so-called hyper-grace community and preach the same message of grace. Do they? To a large degree the answer is yes. Although there are differences of opinion on some points, there is a general consensus as to what constitutes the gospel of grace, as we shall see.

I should add that while Dr. Brown calls it the "modern grace message," those who preach it consider it anything but. The gospel of grace is the ancient and eternal gospel (Rev. 14:6). It is the good news of God's grace that has been broadcast to humanity from before Adam took his first breath.

I should also add that the label "hyper-grace preacher" is one that has been given to us by our critics. It is not how we see ourselves — although that may change as some are coming to embrace this term. Most of the time we refer to ourselves as grace preachers or gospel preachers or simply Christians. When we speak of the grace of God, we typically use phrases like pure grace and radical grace rather than hyper-grace. However, in the hope of promoting engagement, in this book I will embrace the labels Dr. Brown has given us. From here on, I will refer to the gospel of grace as either the modern grace message or the hyper-grace gospel.

Why I wrote this book

I appreciate there is a temptation for any preacher or writer to get defensive whenever their message is misrepresented or misunderstood. However, if we live in reaction to our critics there is a danger that we will become distracted from our primary task of proclaiming the gospel. I am sensitive to this issue and it is something I wrestle with.

By the same token, our critics do us a great service by showing us where we have been unclear in presenting the gospel. By drawing attention to areas of misunderstanding and confusion they signal an opportunity to clarify our message, and for this I am grateful.

When Dr. Brown and I first began corresponding about a year ago, he told me that he was working on a book confronting the errors of the hyper-grace gospel. At that time, and influenced by some of the articles I was reading in the Christian media, I imagined that his book would be little more than a hatchet job. However, when it came out I saw that it wasn't. I was impressed that Dr. Brown had taken the time to read many of our books and I was pleased with the way he positioned the debate as "a dispute within the body, a set of strong differences among fellow-believers," which it is.

Dr. Brown's book is also refreshingly free of some of the more hysterical charges laid against us. He doesn't blame us for the rise of the Nazis and the Democrats.

I would have to say that among the group of people who have seen fit to attack the modern grace message and the hyper-grace movement generally, Dr. Brown is among the most congenial and levelheaded. Our emailed exchanges have been amicable and respectful. When he says on page 5 of his book that he is "truly thrilled" to see many believers being liberated by the modern grace message, I believe him. Although I then wonder why he feels the need to challenge that liberating message.

There is no question that Dr. Brown and I have some strong differences of opinion when it comes to the gospel, but we both love Jesus and we both cherish the grace of God. Neither of us would be having this conversation except that we have both been profoundly changed by grace and consequently we feel passionately about the subject. It is not essential for us to agree on everything. The fact is, God's grace is far bigger than we can imagine. I'm not sure anyone has a handle on it. But what is important is that we discuss our different perspectives with mutual regard and gentle words. Only by doing so do we properly honor the One who gave us grace in the first place.

If Dr. Brown speaks for the critics, permit me to speak for the preachers. But please don't imagine us as lawyers bickering across a courtroom. Heaven forbid. Instead, let's see ourselves sitting at

Starbucks and having a chat. Actually, that won't work because Dr. Brown doesn't drink coffee and neither do I.

Okay, forget Starbucks. We're out in the fresh air, sitting at a picnic table laden with wine and bread. Take a seat. Join us. Where should you sit? It makes no difference at all. Whether you think hyper-grace is a heresy or the best thing ever, I hope you will agree that the people in the debate are more important than the debate itself. Jesus didn't die for an idea, a doctrine, or even the gospel itself. He died for people.

So please discard any notions of being in the right group or the wrong group. This isn't about Us versus Them, for we are all one in Christ. We're not the Council of Nicaea dealing with heresies. We're brothers and sisters having a conversation about Jesus and this wonderful thing called grace.

Got it? Good. Now that's all clear, let me answer the question above. Why did I write this book? I didn't write it to prove my critics wrong or because I am jealous for the purity of the gospel. Nor do I have the slightest desire to play doctrinal policeman. I think we all have better things to do than dot our doctrinal i's and cross our theological t's.

I wrote it because the love of Christ compels me to tell you that God is good and His face is shining upon you. You need to know this. You'll be messed up if you don't.

In this book I'm going to do three things. In Part A, I will give you a short introduction to the hyper-grace gospel. I will tell you what it is and what it isn't. Then in Part B, I will look at some of the common misperceptions people have about it. Finally, in Part C, I will respond to Dr. Brown's specific accusations against it. Again, I don't do this to make him look bad, but to make Jesus look good!

My prayer is that as you read this book you will hear Jesus speaking grace over you. My hope is that as you receive His words of love and favor your heart will be filled with great joy and your life will be radically blessed.

PART A: The Hyper-Grace Gospel

Before we get started, we need to get a few things straight. What is grace? And what is *hyper*-grace?

Here's something you may not know about grace: Jesus never defined it. As far as we know, the Lord of grace who came from the throne of grace full of His Father's grace, and from whom we have received grace upon grace, never uttered the word *grace*. But He sure showed it.

Actions speak louder than words. Jesus did not come to preach grace but to *be* grace and He did this by loving unconditionally and forgiving indiscriminately. Jesus hung out with crooks and conmen and hookers and tax-collectors. He ate with sinners and Pharisees and reached out to filthy foreigners. He told stories of radical grace, defended the guilty, and forgave the unrepentant. And in the greatest demonstration of love the world has ever seen, He gave up His life so that through Him we might truly live.

Inspired by the radical love of Christ, the apostle Paul travelled the world preaching the good news of God's grace. Paul may have been the original hyper-grace preacher for he made no distinction between the *gospel of grace* and the *gospel of Christ*. He treated them as one and the same message. "Jesus is the embodiment of grace," said Paul. "All the blessings and favor of God are found in Him" (see Eph. 1:3).[1]

This is how I explained it in *The Gospel in Twenty Questions*:

> Whenever you read the word grace in the Bible, you can substitute the name Jesus and vice versa. Jesus is grace personified. He is Mr. Grace. What does the grace of God look like? It looks like Jesus. What does the grace of God sound like? It sounds like Jesus ... The grace of God comes in many flavors but is ultimately revealed in His Son, Jesus. Jesus is grace, and grace is Jesus.[2]

If grace is Jesus, what is *hyper*-grace? Some would say it's a meaningless phrase, like wet water or sunny sunshine. Others say hyper-grace is greasy grace, which is bad. Still others say it's abundant grace, which is good.

What is hyper-grace?

Surprisingly, those who coined the term seldom define it. You would expect that in a book called *Hyper-grace* we might be told what hyper-grace is, but we're not. Dr. Brown recognizes that the label appeals to some and offends others, so he leaves it up to the reader to decide whether the "modern grace message" is hyper in the good or bad sense of the word (p. xiii).

Dr. Brown's personal view, of course, is that hyper-grace is a dangerous thing. Hyper-grace is grace plus errors. For the sake of discussion, I'll take the opposing view and say that hyper-grace is a good thing. It's extreme grace. It's over-the-top grace. It's grace on steroids. In the words of John it's grace upon grace.

> For from His fullness we have all received, grace upon grace. (John 1:16, ESV)

God isn't cheap when it comes to lavishing His grace upon us. He gives abundantly out of His fullness. God does not give grace in proportion to our needs, but in accordance with His riches (Eph. 1:7). The thirsty man gets to drink from Niagara Falls.

When describing the generosity of God, Jesus often used the phrase *how much more*. "If you who are evil give good gifts to your children, *how much more* will your heavenly Father give good gifts to those who ask Him!" (see Matt. 7:11). When dispensing grace God gives *much more* than what you would give to your own children. You may be the most generous parent in the world, but your heavenly Father is more generous still. In the competition for Best Dad Ever, God comes first and daylight second.

The rushing flood of God's grace is so great that the sandcastle of your sin cannot hinder it. Paul wrote that where sin abounded, grace did *much more* abound:

But where sin increased and abounded, grace (God's un-merited favor) has surpassed it and increased the more and superabounded. (Romans 5:20b, AMP)

The word Paul uses for describing grace — superabounding — is made up of two Greek words: (1) *huper*, from which we get the English prefix hyper, meaning "over, beyond, and above," and (2) *perisseuo*, which means "superabundant (in quantity) or superior (in quality)."[3]

So to say that God's grace is superabundant only takes you halfway to Paul's meaning. "It's more than that," says the apostle of grace. "It's over, beyond, and above superabundant. It's *super*-superabundant. It's *hyper*-hyper-grace." That's not me putting a spin on Paul's words. That's what he actually says.

Some might say, "Don't get carried away. You can have too much of a good thing." Since grace is Jesus, that's like saying you can have too much of Jesus. That's not possible. While you may have too little of the Lord in your life, you cannot have too much.

Let me prove this with a question: How much does God love you? Can you quantify His love for you? You cannot. On a scale of one to the biggest number you can think of, God's love for you is greater still. It's Buzz Lightyear love. It reaches to infinity and beyond.

In the Bible we are challenged to plumb the depths and ascend the heights of Christ's limitless love for us. Paul prayed that we might have the power to

grasp how wide and long and high and deep is the love of Christ, and to know this love that surpasses knowledge ... (Ephesians 3:18b–19)

This is an astonishing request. "May you grasp the ungraspable, comprehend the incomprehensible, and know the unknowable." This is a prayer that can never be fully answered. Try and locate the boundary of Christ's love for you and you will never succeed. His love for you is greater than you can know or imagine.

Again, that's not me spinning Paul's words. That's what he actually says. The love of Christ surpasses knowledge. Trying to wrap your head around His love is like using a thimble to measure the oceans.

A thousand-year-old poem from a Jewish worship leader expresses the vastness of God's love better than I can:

> Could we with ink the ocean fill,
> And were the skies of parchment made,
> Were every stalk on earth a quill,
> And every man a scribe by trade;
> To write the love of God above
> Would drain the ocean dry;
> Nor could the scroll contain the whole,
> Though stretched from sky to sky.[4]

This ancient poem reminds me of an even older song written by another Jewish worship leader:

> Your love, O Lord, reaches to the heavens,
> Your faithfulness to the skies.
> Your righteousness is like the highest mountains,
> Your justice like the great deep. (Psalm 36:5–6)

We can see from Scripture that God's love and grace are hyper; they extend over, beyond, and above what you can conceive or imagine. What you think of when you think of God's love for you is inevitably inferior to what His love really is. So you could say that grace is what we imagine God's love to be like, but hyper-grace is what it actually is.

Think of it like this. Counting the stars in the night sky won't give you an accurate picture of the bigness of the universe. If you live in a dark place you may be able to see several thousand stars. But what you see is such a tiny proportion of the universe, that really you ain't seen nothing. You have actually *not seen* far more than what you *have seen*.

It's like that with grace. You may look at Jesus and say, "I see grace," but no matter how much grace you see, you only have a tiny glimpse of an unimaginably vast reality.

Grace is what we see; hyper-grace is what it is. This is what John and Paul were trying to convey when they spoke of heaped-up, superabounding grace, and love that passes knowledge. It's what Jesus was trying to tell us when He spoke of the *how much mores* of His gracious and generous Father.

The hyper-grace of God cannot be reduced to words or thoughts that fit inside our minds. It's simply too big. The only way we can begin to grasp it is to see the splendor and awesomeness of God that He has revealed to us through His Son Jesus.

Now, let's flip this over. What is the opposite of hyper-grace? And why do some say we go too far in our portrayal of grace?

Alternatives to hyper-grace

This week I happened upon yet another article attacking the hyper-grace message. The author of this article said that those who preach it place a "strong emphasis on grace." Indeed we do. We say grace saves us and grace keeps us. It's grace from start to finish. So what's the problem?

The problem, apparently, is we're not preaching enough law. In the article the word grace appeared nine times, but the word law appeared thirty times indicating a relatively strong emphasis on the latter. The author wrote, "The Law doesn't save us, but it sanctifies us." The grace of God gets you into the kingdom but it's your observance of the Law — with a capital L — which keeps you there, or at least keeps you from upsetting a temperamental God who is intolerant of your sin.

Since hyper-grace opponents don't like to be called legalists, I'll swap the word law for the word works to acknowledge their view that there are things *you must do* to be saved or sanctified. From this we can identify three gospels:

1. Graceless gospel: You are saved by works and sanctified by works
2. Mixed-grace gospel: You are saved by grace but sanctified by works
3. Hyper-grace gospel: You are saved by grace and sanctified by grace

What is a graceless gospel? There's no such thing. It is grace that makes the good news, *good news*. Remove grace and the good news ceases to be good. Someone once said, "Grace isn't the most important thing in Christianity. It's the only thing." Since grace is another word for Jesus, I agree.

What is a mixed-grace gospel? It's the message that you are saved by grace but kept through works. It's the belief that says one of God's blessings (salvation) comes by grace but all the others (holiness, forgiveness, fellowship, etc.) come through works. I call this a partial gospel because it's partly good news. Jesus saved you (that's the good part), but the rest is up to you (that's the not so good part).

And what is the hyper-grace gospel? It's Jesus plus nothing. It's Christ alone. It's the announcement that Jesus is the author and perfecter of your faith and that He will keep you and present you as faultless to Himself (Heb. 12:2, Jude 1:24). To quote Watchman Nee, it's the declaration that "from start to finish, He is the One who does it all."[5] In the words of D. Martyn Lloyd-Jones, it's the message that causes you to trust in

> ... grace at the beginning, and grace at the end. So that when you and I come to lie upon our death beds, the one thing that should comfort and help and strengthen us there is the thing that helped us in the beginning. Not what we have been, not what we have done, but the grace of God in Jesus Christ our Lord. The Christian life starts with grace, it must continue with grace, it ends with grace. Grace wondrous grace.[6]

The hyper-grace gospel says all the blessings of God come to us freely as gifts. Forgiveness is a gift. Salvation is a gift. Acceptance is a gift. Righteousness is a gift. Holiness is a gift.

Brennan Manning expressed this perfectly in *The Ragamuffin Gospel*:

> Grace proclaims the awesome truth that all is gift. All that is good is ours not by right but by the sheer bounty of a gracious God.[7]

All the gifts of God are found in Jesus Christ. Indeed, Jesus is *the* Gift (John 3:16). This is why the hyper-grace gospel will always point you to Jesus. Whatever your need, He is your rich supply. In the words of an ancient saint, "He who has the Lord has everything."

Some of the differences between the mixed- and hyper-grace gospels are listed in the Table on the next page. As you can see, the two messages are very different. The former puts the focus on you and your works; the latter puts the focus on Jesus and His grace.

How to recognize a mixed-grace gospel

A mixed-grace gospel combines the unmerited favor of God with the merited wage of human-effort. "You are saved by grace but you maintain your position through right-living," is an example of a mixed-grace message. "God gives you grace so that you can keep His commands," is another. These sorts of messages contain an element of grace but ultimately push you to trust in yourself and your own efforts.

Any mixed-grace message can be recognized by the presence of carrots and sticks. Carrots are the blessings you get for obedience; sticks are the penalties you pay for disobedience.

The modern mixed-grace message offers the following carrots: If you confess, you'll be forgiven; if you do right, you'll be accepted; if you act holy, you'll be holy.

And what happens if you don't do these things? What are the sticks of the mixed-grace message? Fail to perform according to prevailing codes of conduct and you'll lose your forgiveness, you'll lose your fellowship, and, if worse comes to worse, you may lose your salvation.

None of this sounds like good news to me. Yet tragically this is the sort of message that millions of people hear every week. They don't hear about Jesus; they hear about carrots and sticks.

Why do people buy into this mixed-up message? They do it because it seems right and fair to them. Their whole lives they've been told, "If you do good, you'll get good, but if you do bad, you'll get bad." Some people call this living under law. Others call

20 differences between the mixed- and hyper-grace gospels[8]

	Mixed-Grace Gospel	Hyper-Grace Gospel
What is it?	Grace + self-effort; you're saved by grace and kept by works	Grace alone; you're saved by grace and kept by grace
Key words	Try, try harder, requirement, hunger, struggle, obey, wrestle, perform, you	Believe, rest in, yield to, surrender, satisfy, trust, receive, Jesus
The preacher...	Drives you with law (look for carrots and sticks)	Draws you with love (look for gracious invitations)
Grace is...	One of God's many blessings; an important doctrine	All of God's blessings wrapped up in Jesus Christ
Faith is...	Trying to influence God	Trusting what God has said or done
Repentance is...	Turning from sin, usually with sorrow and grief	Turning to God, often with joy; changing your unbelieving mind
Confession is...	Reviewing your sins	Agreeing with God
Forgiveness is...	Maintained through repentance and confession	A done deal; in Christ we are eternally forgiven
Obedience is...	Keeping all of God's commands	The result of abiding in the love of Christ
Sanctification is...	A process (you gotta work at it)	A gift to receive; a fruit to cultivate
Be holy because...	Without holiness, no one will see the Lord; so watch yourself	In Christ, you *are* holy; be who you truly are
The law...	Shows us how to please the Lord	Leads us to Christ so that we might be justified by faith
Sacrifice is...	Giving up stuff for the Lord	The Lord giving Himself for us
God's love is...	Unconditional, with conditions	Unconditional, period
The Holy Spirit's conviction...	Points to your badness; it's fault-finding and rebuke	Points to God's goodness; He leads you into the light
Eternal security hinges on...	Your faithfulness	God's faithfulness
I am first and foremost...	A servant of God	A son of God
How to overcome sin...	Repent, confess, try harder—repeat as necessary	Reckon yourself dead to sin and alive to Christ
More gets done when I...	Work	Rest
This message makes me...	Self-conscious	Christ-conscious

it karma. But it's sowing to reap and it has nothing in common with grace.

This is how Bono describes the difference:

> At the center of all religions is the idea of karma. You know, what you put out comes back to you: an eye for an eye, a tooth for a tooth ... It's clear to me that karma is at the very heart of the universe. I'm absolutely sure of it. And yet, along comes this idea called grace to upend all that "As you reap, so you will sow" stuff. Grace defies reason and logic. Love interrupts, if you like, the consequences of your actions, which in my case is very good news indeed, because I've done a lot of stupid stuff.[9]

Another reason why some buy into a mixed-grace gospel is because they feel obliged to prove their worth to God. "Jesus died for you," they hear. "What will you do for Him?" That's a bad question because there is nothing you can do to compensate Him for His priceless gift. Here is a better question:

> How can I repay the Lord for all His goodness to me?
> (Psalm 116:12, NIV1984)

You cannot repay the Lord for His goodness. It's an insult to even try. What you can do is "lift up the cup of salvation," make a toast to the Lord, and say "Thank you, Jesus!" (see Ps. 116:13).

Bite into any mixed-grace message and you will taste a bitter fruit. You will feel the pressure to perform and smell the fear that comes with failure. You'll make promises to God and then you'll break them. You'll resolve to try harder only to fail again and again. You'll become burned out and bummed out.

Since a mixed-grace message puts the emphasis on you and what you have done, your identity will become defined by your productivity. You will start to think of yourself as God's servant instead of His beloved son or daughter. Worst of all, you will end up distracted from Jesus and fallen from grace.

Don't swallow any poison that comes with a spoonful of grace. And don't subscribe to any message that leads you to trust in yourself and your works instead of Jesus and His. To paraphrase Watchman Nee, "You can try or you can trust and the difference is heaven and hell."[10]

> And if by grace, then it cannot be based on works; if it were, grace would no longer be grace. (Romans 11:6)

You may have heard that God gives us grace in order to do good works, but this is misleading. God does not give you grace so that you can work. He gives you grace because He loves you. Period. Those who receive from the abundance of His grace do indeed work and often they work harder than anyone else, but that's neither here nor there.

The issue is not what you'll do for God but what you'll let Him do for you. Will you trust Him a little bit or will you trust Him the whole way? Does His grace merely get you in the front door or does it keep you safe to the very end?

As Jesus said, the only work that counts is the "work" of believing in the One He has sent (John 6:29). This is the chief takeaway of the hyper-grace gospel.

How to recognize the hyper-grace gospel

The hyper-grace gospel is easy to recognize for it is nothing more than boasting about Jesus — who He is and what He has done and what you can now do because of what He has done. If the message you're hearing causes you to fix your eyes on Jesus, and moves you to shout for joy and give thanksgiving and praise for all He has done, chances are you're hearing the hyper-grace gospel.

While a mixed-grace gospel is recognized by the presence of carrots and sticks, the hyper-grace gospel is marked by invitations. Here's one: "Come to me, all you who are weary and burdened, and I will give you rest" (Matt. 11:28). Here's another: "I want to come in and be with you" (Rev. 3:20).

A mixed-grace gospel *drives* people with the law, but the hyper-grace gospel *draws* people with love. This is how Martin Luther distinguished the two messages:

A lawdriver insists with threats and penalties; a preacher of grace lures and incites with divine goodness and compassion shown to us; for He wants no unwilling works and reluctant services, He wants joyful and delightful services of God.[11]

In a quest for holiness a mixed-grace preacher may preach a little law, a little self-help, or a little pop psychology, but it's all just a flesh trip. In contrast, a hyper-grace preacher preaches Christ alone. Whatever your need, whether it's salvation or sanctification, your supply is found in the One who promises to meet all your needs according to His glorious riches in Christ Jesus (Php. 4:19).

In this world you will have trouble. If you are facing the giants of sickness, poverty, and loss, the last thing you need is religious formulas or trite theology. Your greatest need is for a revelation of Jesus Christ who is Lord above all. When you see the One who is greater than all the giants, your mouth will be filled with laughter and your heart with songs of joy. This is the fruit of the hyper-grace gospel.

But don't take my word for it. Let's hear from some other grace preachers. Look carefully at the following good news announcements. Note the absence of carrots and sticks. See how they all point to the grace of God as revealed in Jesus.

- Paul: "Christ died, was buried, then rose. He reigns!" (see 1 Corinthians 15:3–4,25).

- Martin Luther: "The gospel is nothing else but laughter and joy … This was first spoken unto the Jews; for this laughter was first offered to that people, then having the promises. Now he turneth to the Gentiles, whom he calleth to the partaking of this laughter."[12]

- Spurgeon: "None but Jesus! None but Jesus!"[13]

- Malcolm Smith: "Preaching the gospel, we are announcing the news of the revelation of who God is and how He feels about us. We stand on the street corners of the world shouting the news that God is not the way we thought He was—He loves us! ... This is the greatest news in the world ..."[14]

- Andrew Wommack: "God loves you and is extending forgiveness for your sins. Everything that comes as a result of salvation—like forgiveness, righteousness, healing, deliverance, and prosperity—comes to you by grace through faith. It's not based on your performance, but God's grace."[15]

- Joseph Prince: "The gospel is the gospel of Christ, and everything is about Jesus. It's not the gospel of morality and character, and it definitely isn't the gospel of money and prosperity. But do you know what the gospel does? It produces all of those things. The true gospel of Jesus Christ always produces godliness, holiness, morality, character, provision, health, wisdom, love, peace, joy, and much more. They all flow from the gospel of Jesus Christ."[16]

- Robert Farrar Capon: "If the gospel is about anything, it is about a God who meets us where we are, not where we ought to be."[17]

- Dudley Hall: "Grace is a message of unconditional love from the Father of the universe. It's the free offer of the eternal life. And we can experience it all in the gritty now as well as in the sweet by and by."[18]

- Max Lucado: "Grace is everything Jesus. Grace lives because He does, works because He works, and matters because He matters. He placed a term limit on sin and danced a victory jig in a graveyard. To be saved by grace is to be saved by Him—not by an idea, doctrine, creed, or church membership, but by Jesus himself, who will sweep into heaven anyone who so much as gives Him the nod."[19]

- Jerry Bridges: "We are brought into God's kingdom by grace; we are sanctified by grace; we receive both temporal and spiritual blessings by grace; we are motivated to obedience by grace; we are called to serve and enabled to serve by grace; we receive strength to endure trials by grace; and finally, we are glorified by grace. The entire Christian life is lived under the reign of God's grace."[20]

- Tullian Tchividjian: "The gospel of Jesus Christ announces that because Jesus was strong for you, you're free to be weak. Because Jesus won for you, you're free to lose. Because Jesus was Someone, you're free to be no one. Because Jesus was extraordinary, you're free to be ordinary. Because Jesus succeeded for you, you're free to fail."[21]

- Benjamin Dunn: "The scandal (of the cross) is that though your sin was great, God's love was greater ... It is a scandal of love. We couldn't provide a sacrifice, so God provided one for Himself — in Christ. We couldn't climb to Heaven, so Heaven came to us — in Christ. In Christ we see the grand display of the heavens invading the earth. This scandal is designed to make you blush. Its intention is to make every cell in your body scream with thanksgiving and joyful praise!"[22]

- Judah Smith: "That's the gospel. It's good news for everyone. It's not good news just for people who are already good, for those who are self-controlled and disciplined enough to have all their ducks in a row. It's good news for the people who can't even find their ducks. They haven't seen some of their ducks in years. Their lives are a mess. But they can come to Jesus and find instant acceptance."[23]

- Paul White: "It is grace that saves us and then it is grace that keeps us. *We are defined by grace.* Everything we have is a free gift of God, given to us for Christ's sake."[24]

- Various: "The Son of God became the Son of Man that the sons of men might become the Sons of God."[25]

- Anna Bartlett Warner: "Jesus loves me this I know, for the Bible tells me so."[26]

The hyper-grace gospel is simple. You don't need to read Hebrew or Greek to get it. Nor do you need to go to seminary or Bible school. To paraphrase Joseph Prince, the hyper-grace gospel is so simple it takes theologians to complicate it.[27]

There may be 1001 versions of the mixed-grace gospel but there is only one hyper-grace gospel and it is this: *God loves you*. Simple! The reason I have put so many quotes above is not because this message is hard to grasp but because the love of God is extreme, over-the-top, and utterly hyper. *God loves you*. We will spend eternity unpacking those three little words and exploring the immeasurable reaches of His love. It's what we were made for.

Yet we can make this gospel simpler still. We can go from three words to just one and that word is *Jesus*. Jesus is what the love of God looks like. Jesus is the love of God in action. Jesus is the love of God come down.

The hyper-grace gospel is the revelation of Jesus. It is the announcement that He is the beginning and the end, the first word and the last. It is the confident assurance that He who has begun a good work in you will carry it on unto completion. It is the happy revelation that in Christ, your searching is over and you have found your eternal resting place. In Him, you are already home.

Jesus is the hyper-grace gospel!

The hyper-grace gospel quiz

Growing up we used to play a game around the table called Chinese Whispers. (Some people know this as the game of telephone.) Someone would whisper a message into the ear of the person next to them and that message would then be relayed in whispers around the table. When the last person announced what they had heard, we would laugh because it typically bore little resemblance to the original message.

That's how I feel when I hear some of the criticisms made against the hyper-grace message. It's like the person complaining has heard the message third-hand or only heard part of the message and is criticizing something no one actually said. It's a little bit funny and a little bit sad.

Much of the criticism made against the hyper-grace gospel and those who preach it is based on misperceptions and misunderstandings. To illustrate this, ask yourself whether the following claims are true or false.

1.	Hyper-grace preachers are against repentance.	T	F
2.	Hyper-grace preachers are against confession.	T	F
3.	The hyper-grace gospel is universalism in disguise.	T	F
4.	Hyper-grace preachers say it's wrong to ask God for forgiveness.	T	F
5.	Hyper-grace preachers say God is not grieved by your sin.	T	F
6.	Hyper-grace preachers are against the law.	T	F
7.	Hyper-grace preachers ignore the Old Testament.	T	F
8.	Hyper-grace preachers disregard the words of Jesus.	T	F
9.	The hyper-grace gospel encourages sin.	T	F
10.	The hyper-grace gospel discourages obedience and holy living.	T	F
11.	Hyper-grace preachers don't talk about hell and wrath.	T	F
12.	The hyper-grace gospel makes people lazy.	T	F

To have real dialogue, you need to hear both sides of the story. If your only exposure to the hyper-grace gospel comes from attack articles and Facebook debates, you may think that every statement in the above quiz is true. In fact, every statement is false. Each is either a fiction or a distortion of what the hyper-grace gospel actually says. We will look at each claim briefly in Part B.

PART B: 12 Myths about the Hyper-Grace Gospel

Myth 1: Hyper-grace preachers are against repentance

"Hyper-grace preachers say there's no need for repentance. They dismiss repentance as unbelief." Actually, hyper-grace preachers are *for* repentance, not against it. We say things like "repentance is essential" and "repentance is to be our lifestyle." We are for repentance, for without it no one can receive the grace of God.

But what is repentance?

Repentance is one of those words that means different things to different people. Those with a performance-oriented mindset typically interpret repentance as turning from sin. It's something you do (turn) as a result of something you've done (sinned). It's fixing what you broke. It's atoning for your mistakes. It's sewing fig leaves to hide your shame.

In contrast, faith-based repentance is always done in response to something *God* has done. It's the change of heart and mind that happens when you encounter His grace.

A mixed-grace gospel will define repentance in terms of a prescribed set of behaviors (e.g., turning from sin) and emotions (e.g., sorrow and grief). But insisting on the proper way to repent is tantamount to putting people under law.

The fruit of repentance may take 101 different forms—don't limit God—but repentance itself is simply a change of mind. It's what the word literally means.[1]

In the words of Watchman Nee:

Repentance ... means a change of mind! Formerly I thought sin a pleasant thing, but now I have changed my mind about it; formerly I thought the world an attractive place, but now I know better; formerly I regarded it a miserable business to be a Christian, but now I think differently. Once I thought certain things delightful, now I think them vile; once I thought other things utterly worthless, now I think them most precious. That is a change of mind, and that is repentance. No life can be truly changed apart from such a change of mind.[2]

We all agree that repentance is a good thing and that there should be more of it, but how do we get people to repent? A mixed-grace preacher will use carrots ("Turn from sin if you want to see God") and sticks ("If you don't, you'll pay the price"), but this is the way of the flesh, not faith. This sort of repentance will lead you to trust in your own repenting efforts and miss grace. Consider the Pharisees. They turned from sin on a daily basis yet they did not recognize the Grace of God even as He came and stood among them.

Mixed-grace preachers say, "We need more preaching on repentance," as though this would motivate people to repent. But it won't. Only one thing is guaranteed in Scripture to lead people to repentance and that is a revelation of God's goodness:

> ... God's kindness is meant to lead you to repentance.
> (Romans 2:4b, ESV)

Repentance isn't doing something about your sin. Repentance is responding positively to God's kindness and grace. Think of Zacchaeus, the corrupt tax-collector. The Grace of God walked into his home and he became a different man.

John Sheasby explains it like this:

> The goodness in Jesus' spirit created a comfortable, safe environment in which, though there was no pressure to change, Zacchaeus found himself wanting to and choosing to change. The goodness of God expressed in Jesus produced a true repentance.[3]

How does a hyper-grace preacher encourage repentance? By preaching the goodness of God as revealed in Jesus. A mixed gospel says, "You gotta repent or else," but the hyper-grace gospel says, "See Jesus!" Old covenant repentance puts the focus on you and your badness, but new covenant repentance puts the focus on Him and His goodness.

When you see the Lord of grace looking at you with love and affection, you will repent. You will turn from sin to Him not because you have been bribed with carrots or threatened with sticks but because Jesus is more attractive than anything this world offers. He is the Beauty who draws us to Himself.

When Jesus said "Repent and believe the good news" (Mark 1:15), He was saying "Here is the good news of God's grace — change your skeptical mind and believe it." If you want to see more repentance, preach the good news of God's kindness. Tell people about the goodness of God that is found in Jesus.

Myth 2: Hyper-grace preachers are against confession

"Hyper-grace preachers say it's wrong to confess sins. They say confession is a form of unbelief." Actually, every hyper-grace preacher believes in the power of confession. We say things like, "confession is good for you," and "confession is healthy." But what is confession?

Like the word repentance, confession is a word that has been mangled in the machinery of manmade religion. Instead of bringing healing to the hurting and life to the dead, confession is seen as the cost of admission into the house of grace. "You wanna be clean? Then 'fess up you miserable sinner! Tell God your dirty little secrets." But that's not what confession is.

To confess literally means to agree with or say the same thing as another.[4] Biblical confession is agreeing with God. It's verbalizing faith in His goodness and acknowledging your dependence upon Him (Rom. 10:9–10). It's saying, "God, I believe You are faithful and true and will do all that You promised."

But some people have a different definition of confession. They think confession is something *you must do* to make yourself clean, righteous, and forgiven. "I have to review all my sins to receive forgiveness." But this is a dead work. Confessing-to-be-forgiven is like washing with dirty water. No matter how hard you scrub you won't make yourself clean.

Faithless confession puts the focus on you and what you have done, but faith-based confession puts the focus on Christ and what He has done on your behalf.

Does that mean we should never confess or that it's wrong to confess our sins? Not at all. Biblical confession is good for you. It will help you to walk in the grace that God has provided.

Steve McVey writes:

> Is there a place for confession in the Christian's life? Yes, if confession means acknowledging the foolishness of disobedience to the Father and then praising Him that we are *already* forgiven and accepted by Him.[5]

One of the clearest descriptions of confession comes from Max Lucado:

> Confession is not complaining. If I merely recite my problems and rehash my woes, I'm whining ... Confession is so much more. Confession is a radical reliance on grace. A proclamation of our trust in God's goodness. "What I did was bad," we acknowledge, "but your grace is greater than my sin, so I confess it." If our understanding of grace is small, our confession will be small: reluctant, hesitant, hedged with excuses and qualifications, full of fear of punishment. But great grace creates an honest confession.[6]

We don't repent and confess to get God to forgive us. We repent and confess *because* God has forgiven us. Your repentance and confession won't change God, but it will surely change you. It will help you receive God's life-changing grace. As Clark Whitten says, "Confession is for my healing, not for God's forgiveness."[7]

Those who don't understand this may point to 1 John 1:9 which seems to say God's forgiveness is contingent upon our confession of sins. This scripture has been so widely misunderstood that it gets mentioned in just about every book on grace. To paraphrase Andrew Farley, John cannot be saying God forgives us on account of our confession because just a few verses later he says we are forgiven on account of Jesus' name.[8] (We'll take a closer look at 1 John 1:9 in Part C.)

When you sin it takes no faith to beat yourself up and agree with the Accuser who calls you a sinner. It takes faith to look at the cross and say, "Thank you, Jesus, for carrying all my sin." It takes faith to praise your Father for His superabounding grace that is greater than your transgression. And it takes faith to agree with the Holy Spirit who says, despite what you did, you are still righteous, acceptable, and pleasing to God.

Myth 3: The hyper-grace gospel is universalism in disguise

"The hyper-grace gospel says all will be saved." Actually, it says no such thing. The hyper-grace gospel is an announcement of something that has happened. It's not speculation about something that may yet happen.

Because I preach the unconditional love of God and universal forgiveness, I am often accused of being a Universalist. A Universalist is someone who believes all will be saved. While it may be true that most Universalists preach grace, it is not true that most grace-preachers are Universalists. In my experience, the majority are not.

So why are hyper-grace preachers mistaken for Universalists? It may be because we say the whole world is forgiven.

"See, that's universalism right there. You're saying everyone is saved." Only I'm not. Forgiveness doesn't equal salvation. Forgiveness simply means God won't judge you for your sins. How can He, since He has already judged all your sins on the cross (Rom. 8:3)?

Your sins are not the issue. *Jesus* is the issue. It's what you have done with *Him* that counts. Since there are some who reject the grace of God revealed in Jesus, I do not think everyone will be saved. In the end everyone gets what they want. If you want the life Jesus offers, you'll have it. If you don't, you won't.

But let's return to this business of universal forgiveness. Why do I say the whole world is forgiven? Because that's what the Bible says. John the Baptist said of Jesus, "Behold the Lamb of God who takes away the sin of *the world*" (John 1:29). To take away sin is to forgive. It's what the word forgive literally means. It's to send away, dismiss, forsake, and let go.[9]

On the cross, Jesus took away your sin. Your sin is no longer the problem. It was a problem, but Jesus dealt with it once and for all time. By His sacrifice Jesus has "done away with sin" (Heb. 9:26).

On the cross Jesus became:

> ... the propitiation for our sins, and not for ours only but also
> for the sins of the whole world. (1 John 2:2, ESV)

Jesus didn't just take away the sins of repentant, church-goers. He
took away the sins of tax collectors and tax dodgers, hookers and
hackers, phonies and Pharisees. He bore everyone's sin.

Jesus said, "For God so loved the world." As Dudley Hall has
written, God doesn't just love good guys; He loves everyone in the
world.

> If you live in the world, perfect love is offered to you. It is not
> offered only to the good.[10]

If God's love is indiscriminate, then so is His forgiveness. This is
the true message of the cross.

Before the cross, Jesus preached conditional forgiveness to
those who were born under the old covenant law (e.g., Matt. 6:14–
15), but on the cross He fulfilled all the requirements of the law so
that you might live under the new covenant of His grace. On the
night He rose from the dead, Jesus announced a new kind of
forgiveness (Luke 24:46–47): Forgiveness that is based on God's
favor rather than your works.[11]

The gospel declares that through Christ you have been completely and eternally forgiven. This is amazing news. Yet as
Malcolm Smith has observed, most Christians haven't heard it.

> There is no other religion on earth that announces the forgive-
> ness of all our sins ... Our assurance that our sins have been
> forgiven and we have been accepted by God is the first of
> covenant blessings and the most important in our experience.
> Without this, we cannot imagine any of the other blessings.
> This is the kindergarten of the new covenant, yet for
> multitudes of church members such a joy has not been even
> sighted.[12]

The unsighted joy of God's forgiveness keeps many Christians
busy pursuing that which they already possess. They hear muddled messages like, "Jesus paid for your sins but He hasn't for-

given you," and they are told, "you need to repent and confess to complete the transaction." But the gospel of grace announces:

> Forgiveness precedes repentance. The sinner is accepted before He pleads for mercy. It is already granted. He need only receive it. Total amnesty. Gratuitous pardon.[13]

What is true for the sinner is true for the saint. You are loved! You are forgiven! God is not chasing you with a scorebook. He pursues you with grace.

There is nothing you can do to make God forgive you because He's already done it. Your sins have been removed "as far as the east is from the west" (Ps. 103:12). Because of Jesus, God is no longer counting your sins against you. This is the hyper-grace gospel!

Myth 4: Hyper-grace preachers say it's wrong to ask God for forgiveness

"Beware the grace Pharisees who jump on you if you say something that smacks of unbelief in grace. They say it's a sin to ask God for forgiveness."

There is nothing wrong in coming to the throne of grace in your hour of need to receive mercy and find grace. If you need forgiveness, God has an ample supply. If asking helps you to receive, then ask. It's not wrong to ask. What's *wrong* is telling people God won't forgive them unless they first do things like repent or confess all their sins. What's *wrong* is telling the poor and needy they've got to pay to dine at the table of the Lord's abundance. What's *wrong* is putting price tags on the free gift of grace.

It's not wrong to ask God for anything. He's your Father and He cares for you. He wants you to present all your requests to Him (Php. 4:6). If you have made mistakes and are in need of forgiveness, have the freedom to ask knowing that He will give you what you ask for.

But here's something you may not appreciate: God will forgive you even if you *don't* ask. How do I know? Because He's already done it.

> In Him we have redemption through His blood, the forgiveness of sins, in accordance with the riches of God's grace. (Ephesians 1:7)

Perhaps you think you *have* to ask for forgiveness as in, "If I don't ask, God won't forgive me." That's like saying, "Christ didn't carry all my sin," which He did, or "Jesus needs to come and die again," which He won't, or "God needs my permission to forgive me," which He doesn't.

Writing in *The Naked Gospel,* Andrew Farley says asking God to forgive you is like asking your wife to marry you. It might help you confirm in your mind that you are actually married, but it's not necessary. Whether you ask or not won't change the fact that you are married. Similarly, asking God for forgiveness won't change the fact you are forgiven.

Farley notes that nowhere in the New Testament epistles is there any hint that we need to ask God to forgive us.

> Why not? Because the writers penned their words *after* the death of Jesus. They were fully aware of their forgiveness as an accomplished fact.[14]

By all means have the freedom to repent, confess, ask, say sorry, or turn cartwheels if you wish, but do these things out of a sense of gratitude rather than obligation. Understand that you are not forgiven because you *did the right things* or *asked in the proper manner.* You are forgiven because your Father loves you and abounds in grace towards you.

Joseph Prince writes:

> I have nothing against saying "sorry" to God or confessing our sins ... Do I say "sorry" to God and confess my sins when I have fallen short and failed? Of course I do. But I do it not to

be forgiven because I *know* that I am *already* forgiven through Jesus' finished work.[15]

From God's side, forgiveness is a done deal. There remain no more sacrifices for sin. But from our side sin may be a big problem indeed. Many are crippled by guilt and condemnation. Others remain slaves to sin and are incapable of making healthy choices. The solution is not to buy into a message of dead works—"Try harder! Turn from sin! Beg God to forgive you!" The remedy is to receive the grace that has been provided in Jesus Christ.

Why do you need to receive the gift of forgiveness if you are already forgiven? For the same reason you need to receive the grace of God that has appeared to all people; it will change you. It will free you from sin's brutal and condemning grip.

Unwanted grace is worthless. Leave God's grace on the shelf and it won't benefit you. This is why the New Testament writers exhort us to believe the good news. They're basically saying, "Quit beating yourself up over sin and trying to make yourself clean. Trust Jesus and rest in His finished work."

Receiving grace is simply a matter of agreeing with God. It's thanking Him that through Jesus "I have been cleansed from all unrighteousness, and all my sins have been taken away."

Myth 5: Hyper-grace preachers say God is not grieved by your sin

"Hyper-grace preachers say God doesn't care when we sin." Actually, we say God cares very much because sin hurt the objects of His affection—us! Sin damages people, fractures friendships, and destroys families. Sin hurts you, and that makes your Father sad.

> And do not grieve the Holy Spirit of God, with whom you were sealed for the day of redemption. Get rid of all bitterness, rage and anger, brawling and slander, along with every form of malice. Be kind and compassionate to one another, forgiving each other, just as in Christ God forgave you.
> (Ephesians 4:30–32)

33

Is God oblivious to our shortcomings and sins? When you sin does He act like Sergeant Schulz and say, "I see nothing"? Of course not. God sees everything. Our choices bring Him pleasure and pain. Paul would not have written, "Do not grieve the Holy Spirit of God" if that wasn't possible.

But you need to understand *why* God is grieved. He's not grieved because you disappoint Him. (Since He knows everything you've ever done and will ever do, it's not possible to disappoint Him.) Nor is He grieved because you broke His rules. (You are worth more to Him than any rule.) Our sins grieve Him because they hurt His kids.

Look at the sins Paul lists above and you will see they are all relational sins. They are the sins of quarreling, backbiting, and being a jerk. When we act this way we hurt those closest to us and make our Father sad. When we sin out of anger, says Paul, we give place to the devil and open a door to trouble (Eph. 4:26–27). That doesn't make your Father happy and it won't make you happy either.

Critics of the hyper-grace gospel say things like, "Grace teaches that God turns a blind eye to our sin." It would be more accurate to say, "Grace teaches that God chooses to remember our sins no more." But that doesn't mean our sins don't trouble Him. He is our loving Father. He cares deeply for us. He is not happy to see us destroy ourselves through sin.

If Jesus didn't care about the effects of sin, He would not have gone to the cross. Nor would He have warned the churches in Revelation about their bad behavior and unhealthy habits. The gospel declares that God's love is unaffected by our choices, but it does not follow that we can act without consequences.

Your behavior matters to God because *you* matter to God. He wants you to prosper and thrive in every area of your life. He doesn't want you opening the door to trouble by sowing to the flesh. But even if you do—even if you make one dumb mistake after another—He will still be your Father and you will still be His dearly loved child. Your actions may be harmful and saddening to Him but *you* will always be the apple of His eye.

If you don't understand the hyper-grace gospel you may imagine the Holy Spirit to be the sheriff of heaven recording all your sins and convicting you when you're guilty. You may see Him as a Prosecutor and Policeman even though Jesus called Him the Comforter and Counselor.

Act like a sinner and you'll grieve the Holy Spirit, but here's what won't happen: The Holy Spirit won't record your sins, for He promised not to (Heb. 10:15–17); nor will He send you on a guilt-trip, for He's the Spirit of grace not the Spirit of guilt; and He won't withdraw from you until you get your act together, for Jesus said He would never leave you (John 14:16).

When you sin, the Holy Spirit will always point you to Jesus. He knows that as we behold the kindness and compassion of Jesus, we become kind and compassionate ourselves. As we gaze at His forgiving face, we become forgiving. As we marvel at His beauty, we become beautiful. As we behold Jesus we are transformed into His shining testimonies of grace. This makes the Holy Spirit happy.

Myth 6: Hyper-grace preachers are against the law

"Hyper-grace preachers claim that God's law is bad or defective," say the critics. "They are opposed to His holy commands."

Hyper-grace preachers are accused of being antinomian or against the law because we preach what Paul preached; that we are not under law but grace (Rom. 6:14–15). We say that Christ is the end of the law for all who believe (Rom. 10:4).

The charge of antinomianism is an old one. As Clark Whitten has observed, religious people have been accusing grace preachers of being opposed to the law ever since Jesus showed up:

Jesus must have been accused of being antinomian because He defended himself by saying, "Do not think that I came to abolish the law or the prophets; I did not come to abolish but to fulfill" (Matt. 5:17). Apostle Paul must have heard the same antinomian accusation from the Judaizers and responded by writing the book of Galatians![16]

35

Are hyper-grace preachers against the law? Not at all. We are 100 percent for the law and the purpose for which it was given. Joseph Prince speaks for all of us when he writes:

> One of the things I have been accused of is being an anti-nomian (someone who is against the law of Moses). The truth is that I have the highest regard for the law ... I am for the law, for the purpose for which God gave the law ... God did not give the law for us to keep. He gave the law to bring man to the end of himself, so that he would see his need for a Savior.[17]

A mixed-grace gospel mixes law with grace and reaps the benefits of neither. It promotes the law as a guide for living and treats grace as little more than a lubricant for greasing the cogs of self-effort. Those who buy into this message reveal their disregard for both law, since they cannot keep it yet pretend to, and grace, since they would rather trust in their own efforts than in Christ's magnificent work. Such a person is lukewarm. They have not yielded to either the cold and unbending demands of the law or the white-hot love and grace of their Father.

In contrast, those who preach a hyper-grace gospel esteem the law and agree with Paul who said "the law is good if one uses it properly" (see 1 Tim. 1:8–11). We understand that the law is made not for the righteous but for lawbreakers and those opposed to the gospel. The law is for those who trust in themselves and their own righteousness rather than in Christ and His.

A mixed-grace preacher will tell you that the law shows you how to please the Lord, but it doesn't. *Faith* pleases the Lord and the law is not of faith (Gal. 3:12).

A mixed-grace preacher will say, "God gave us the law to help you overcome sin," but He didn't. God gave us the law to help sin overcome you (Rom. 7:10–11). As Watchman Nee once said,

> We can say, reverently, that God never gave us the Law to keep: He gave us the Law to break! He well knew that we could not keep it.[18]

36

A hyper-grace preacher understands that the purpose of the law is to reveal sin so that we might see our need for a Savior (Rom. 7:7).

> So the law was put in charge to lead us to Christ that we might be justified by faith. Now that faith has come, we are no longer under the supervision of the law.
> (Galatians 3:24–25, NIV1984)

The law was put in charge to bring us to the end of ourselves so that we might see our need for grace. Therefore, the real antinomians are those who use the law for other purposes. They are those who honor the law with their lips while keeping only some of the commands. They are the mixed-grace preachers who dilute the law's power to condemn the proud and silence the self-righteous. And they are the lawdrivers who dare to threaten Christ's bride with curses and penalties.

Myth 7: Hyper-grace preachers ignore the Old Testament

"Hyper-grace preachers would have you throw away most of your Bible," say the critics. "They dismiss the Old Testament as irrelevant and useless." This is not true. We view the Old Testament as a treasure trove of stories, songs, statutes, prophecies, and promises that all point to Jesus.

The misperception that hyper-grace preachers ignore the Old Testament is easily refuted. Just read our books, watch our sermons, or listen to our podcasts. Take Joseph Prince for example. If you have heard him preach, you will know that he mines the riches of the Old Testament like few can. He delves into the meanings of Hebrew words, obscure passages, and old stories to show how the coming of Jesus and the release of God's grace was eagerly anticipated by those who lived before Him.

> You can preach from Genesis to Revelation from the perspective of Jesus and His grace … After all, Christ is in the Old Testament concealed, and in the New Testament revealed.[19]

The Old Testament is epic in scope. It covers the long period between the creation of the world and the arrival of Jesus. Somewhere in the middle of that period, Moses led the children of Israel to Mt. Sinai where they signed up for the old covenant. This was the law-keeping covenant that ran for fourteen centuries and was fulfilled on the cross. The New Testament writers make it plain that we are not to live under this old or obsolete covenant because Jesus has forged a new and better covenant based on His grace (Heb. 8:13).

The old and new covenants are very different. The old was based on frequent animal sacrifices that could never take away sin, while the new is based on the once-for-all-time sacrifice of the spotless Lamb of God (Heb. 9:26, 10:4). The old hung on your obedience and was thus doomed to fail, while the new rests on Christ's perfect obedience unto death and thus has already succeeded.

The two covenants can be distinguished in terms of their language. Those who lived under the old covenant spoke with hunger and unfulfilled longing as they looked forward to Jesus. But we who live under the new covenant look back with gratitude and speak a new language of thanksgiving and praise. We say things like, "I have been crucified with Christ," and "I am a new creation." Or we would, if we understood the significance of the cross.

Benjamin Dunn writes:

> Isn't it heart-rending that so many believers don't know how to speak this (new) language? They are stuck in the undone, instead of floating upon the finished. Some of the phrases of the old language are: "I must nail myself to the cross every day." "I'm just a sinner saved by grace." "Lord, You saved me but now come and cleanse me," or "Every day I've got to die to my flesh." Obviously the list goes on, and for the sheer fact that I hate hearing them, I will say no more of these faithless jabberings. This is a dead language![20]

We are not to live by the old covenant, but that doesn't mean we should rip it out of our Bibles. As long as we read the old with the eyes of the new we will see what we are supposed to see:

> And beginning with Moses and all the Prophets, He explained to them what was said in all the Scriptures concerning Himself. (Luke 24:27)

Jesus preached from the Old Testament so that His disciples might see what was said concerning Himself. That's why we read the Bible — to see Jesus. There are pictures of Jesus on every page.

The Bible is a story about Jesus who loved us, lost us, and won us back. It tells this story a thousand different ways, and this is why hyper-grace preachers don't want you to throw away parts of your Bible. All of it is good and all of it points to Jesus. The Bible is the greatest story ever told.

Myth 8: Hyper-grace preachers disregard the words of Jesus

"Hyper-grace preachers say the words of Jesus are not for us. They have no authority and are irrelevant to the modern church."

One of the strangest claims made against hyper-grace preachers is that we are dismissive of the pre-cross teachings of Jesus. In point of fact, hyper-grace preachers are the only ones taking Jesus seriously. When Jesus is preaching law, we say that's authentic law, not to be taken lightly. And when Jesus is revealing grace, we bow in awestruck gratitude. We would not dare to re-interpret His words with qualifiers and caveats.

In contrast, those who preach a mixed-grace message dismiss the hard words of Jesus as hyperbole and exaggeration. "Jesus didn't mean what He said about chopping off limbs or being perfect." Like the Pharisees of old, they pick and choose those commands which are to be followed while disregarding others as metaphorical, unreal, and not to be taken seriously.

To be fair, the misperception that hyper-grace preachers reject the teachings of Jesus is based on a kernel of truth, which is this: Everything Jesus said is good, but not everything Jesus said is good for you. Or to put it another way, Jesus spoke words the whole world needs to hear, but you are not the whole world.

For instance, Jesus had strong words for the Pharisees whom He called snakes and sons of hell (Matthew 23:15, 33). Are you a snake? Are you a son of hell? If not, then Jesus words for them may not be meant for you.

Does this mean we should go through the Gospels cutting out those bits that don't apply to us? Personally, I don't like the idea of chopping up the Bible. I think all Scripture is useful for teaching and training in righteousness (2 Tim. 3:16). But relevance is determined by context.

If you are self-righteous, then the harsh words of Jesus to the self-righteous are relevant for you. You need to hear Jesus say this:

> For I tell you that unless your righteousness surpasses that of the Pharisees and the teachers of the law, you will certainly not enter the kingdom of heaven. (Matthew 5:20)

However, if you are not confident of your own righteousness, then you need to hear His promises of grace:

> Blessed are those who hunger and thirst for righteousness, for they will be filled. (Matthew 5:6)

What you hear in the words of Jesus reflects what is in your heart. If you are standing on your own righteousness you will hear law like you've never heard it before. "You have heard it said ... but I say unto you ..."

Jesus preached tough, merciless law that leaves no margin for error. "Be perfect as your heavenly Father is perfect" (Matt. 5:48). The message is clear. Either you must be perfect or you must be represented by One who is.

However, if you already know that you are not perfect, you need to hear Jesus' words of grace. You need to hear Him speak about His Father who loves you, cares for you, and offers you His righteousness (Matt. 6:33).

The genius of Jesus is that He could speak to a crowd of people and connect with everyone at their point of need. Consider Jesus' story of the Pharisee and the tax collector (Luke 18:9–14):

How does this parable make you feel? Does it fill you with joy or resentment? Your response to the story is your response to the gospel. If you identify with the sinful tax collector, then this story is good news. *Really? He went home justified?* That's the scandal of grace right there. God justifies sinners (Romans 4:5) ... But if you are confident of your self-righteousness, this story is not good news at all. "Wait a second. I fast. I tithe. I am better than other people. Jesus, what are you saying?" Jesus doesn't mince His words. "Everyone who exalts himself will be humbled" (Luke 18:14). That's a hard word for a hard heart. It's a word that condemns the self-righteous and silences the boastful. It's a word of law for those who don't see their need for grace.[21]

A mixed-grace preacher reads the words of Jesus selectively but a hyper-grace preacher values everything Jesus says. He recognizes that Jesus is the perfect Physician who always prescribes the perfect medicine. He gives law to the smug and grace to the needy. No matter who you are or where you are on your journey, Jesus has life-saving words for you.

Myth 9: The hyper-grace gospel encourages sin

"The hyper-grace gospel leads people to sin. Sinful living is the fruit of the modern grace message." For 2,000 years, those opposed to the gospel of grace have said it promotes sin and licentiousness (Romans 6:1–2). But grace is no more a license to sin than electricity is a license to electrocute yourself. Saying "grace promotes sin" is like saying "medicine promotes sickness." It's a distortion that leads people to distrust the only thing that can empower them to sin no more.

Spurgeon had little time for such foolishness:

No doctrine is so calculated to preserve a man from sin as the doctrine of the grace of God. Those who have called it "a licentious doctrine" did not know anything about it.[22]

"Hyper-grace preachers say it doesn't matter what you do. You can go on sinning." Actually, it does matter what you do because sin is destructive. Sin hurts people. But since we are not in the habit of drawing attention to other people's sin, I can understand how some have this misperception. So can D. Martyn Lloyd-Jones:

There is no better test as to whether a man is really preaching the New Testament gospel of salvation than this, that some people might misunderstand it and misinterpret it to mean that it really amounts to this, that because you are saved by grace alone it does not matter at all what you do; you can go on sinning as much as you like because it will redound all the more to the glory of grace. That is a very good test of gospel preaching. If my preaching and presentation of the gospel of salvation does not expose it to that misunderstanding, then it is not the gospel.[23]

Preach the scandalous grace of God and some will misinterpret your message as an endorsement of sin. It's practically inevitable. But those who dismiss grace as a license to sin merely show their ignorance of it. As John Calvin may have said, "How can the medicine that's supposed to kill the disease (grace) feed the disease (sin)?"

"Hyper-grace preachers are soft on sin. They don't condemn the sin that's right in front of them." The same accusation could be leveled at Jesus. An adulterous woman was brought to Him for judgment and He didn't even mention her sin. Not once. Instead, He said "go and sin no more" (John 8:11). Jesus wasn't making a threat. He was saying, "Receive my gift of no condemnation and be set free from sin."

"Hyper-grace preachers are closet sinners who distort the message of grace to accommodate their ungodly lifestyles." Grace preachers are sometimes compared to the licentious men of Jude 1:4. Because we stand with Jesus instead of the rock-throwing

Pharisees we are thought to be soft on sin and sinners ourselves. This is a slanderous accusation made by the ignorant and grace-less.

To be sure, the abuse of grace is a legitimate concern. But so is medical malpractice and no one is suggesting we should shut down hospitals. As Rob Rufus likes to say, "The best response to abuse is not non-use but proper use."

Grace-abusers are often confused about their relationship to God. As Jefferson Bethke has said, "Only people who see God as their judge, not their Father, try to take advantage of grace."[24]

The issue for the abuser is not behavior but identity, because one follows the other. What you do flows out of who you are. If you see yourself as a sinner, you'll sin. But if you see yourself as a dearly loved child of God, you won't. You'll gladly receive His grace that frees you from the dominion of sin (see Rom. 6:14).

Paul White writes:

There is a difference between chasing grace for what it gives and chasing it for Who grace is ... It is Jesus, not a message, that makes us who we are.[25]

Jesus is grace. To abuse grace is to abuse Jesus. Those who love Him would never do it.

For the grace of God has appeared that offers salvation to all people. It teaches us to say "No" to ungodliness ...
(Titus 2:11–12a)

Jesus is the grace of God that offers salvation to all people. His grace teaches us to say no to sin. If the grace you're drinking teaches you to say yes to sin, it's not the grace of God. It's a man-made substitute.

To say grace promotes sin is like saying Jesus promotes sin. It's slanderous at best, and blasphemous at worst. Grace isn't per-mission to sin; it's the power of God to sin no more.

Some make a great show of suppressing sin by laying down the law but all they do is drive sin underground. A law-based approach cannot work because the strength of sin is the law (1 Cor.

15:56). Combating sin with the law is like trying to put out a fire with a bucket of gasoline.

It is not God's law that teaches us to say no to ungodliness, it is His grace. Those who seek to mix grace with law ruin the medicine that would otherwise set you free. Only God's pure and undiluted grace can turn a sinner into a saint, a hater into a lover, and a Pharisee into an apostle.

Stumble and sin in a mixed-grace church and the message you get will be, "Look at what you did!" But sin in a hyper-grace church and the message will be, "Look at what He did and what you can now do because of what He did!"

A mixed-grace church would have you turn from every sin until you're a dizzy sinner. But a hyper-grace church will do what Paul did with the sinning Corinthians and seek to reveal your true identity in Christ. They will say things like·

> (You are) sanctified in Christ Jesus and called to be His holy people ... Grace and peace to you from God our Father and the Lord Jesus Christ. I always thank God for you because of His grace given you in Christ Jesus. For in Him you have been enriched in every way ... (and) He will also keep you firm to the end, so that you will be blameless on the day of our Lord Jesus Christ. (1 Corinthians 1:2–5, 8).

We don't get victory over sin by striving to keep the rules. We overcome sin by trusting Jesus who loves us and lives within. So reckon yourself dead to sin and alive to Christ and be free!

Myth 10: The hyper-grace gospel discourages obedience and holy living

"Grace preachers may not be promoting sin," say the critics. "But neither are they challenging people to embrace a lifestyle of obedience to Jesus." That depends on your definition of obedience. If by obedience you mean, "Obey the rules, or else," then you are right for a grace preacher would put law on a believer.

A mixed-grace preacher says, "You gotta obey God," but the bottom line is not whether you obey Him, but whether you trust

Him. Wayne Jacobsen explains the difference in his book, *He Loves Me*:

> One can obey God and yet not trust Him, and in doing so miss out on a relationship with Him. One cannot, however, trust God and be disobedient to Him.[26]

Grace preachers emphasize the love of God for the same reason Jesus did: Our Father's love is the root on which we grow. Obedience is not something we do to merit His love. It is evidence that His love has been made complete in us.

Joseph Prince writes:

> People say that those who preach grace don't preach on obedience. What they don't realize is that under the old covenant of law, obedience was the root of all God's blessings. But under the new covenant of grace God blesses us first, and obedience is the fruit.[27]

Another complaint made against the hyper-grace gospel is that it is unbalanced. It emphasizes one teaching (grace) above all others (repentance, obedience, holiness, etc.). But as we have seen, grace is not a teaching. Grace is a Person and His name is Jesus. In Him is found all the wisdom and all the teaching you'll ever need.

Others say, "we need grace *and* we need truth," as though it was possible to have one without the other. Yet there is no grace without truth and both are embodied in Jesus. "Grace and truth came through Jesus Christ" (John 1:17). If you have Him you have grace *and* you have truth in abundance. You have the complete package.

But for the sake of argument, let's say you could have grace without truth. What is the truth that is apparently missing from the hyper-grace gospel? According to our critics, it is an insufficient emphasis on law keeping and holy living.

"The hyper-grace preachers say, 'Jesus loves you,' but that's only half the message. They don't tell you about His words in John 14:15 — 'If you love me, you will obey what I command.'"

A mixed-grace preacher reads the words of Jesus backwards and says you must obey to prove your love. But obedience is a fruit, not a root. Jesus is making a promise not a threat. He's saying that as you abide in the vine and bask in His love, He will bear His fruit in your life effortlessly. It's inevitable.

A hyper-grace preacher takes Jesus at His word: "If you love me, you will obey." Those who are resting in the unconditional love of Jesus will trust Him and do what He says without any conscious effort. They don't need rules to tell them what to do for the Holy Spirit Himself is their guide (John 16:13). It's a completely different way to live.

"Hyper-grace preachers affirm the lustful desires of their hearers." What lustful desires? If you've been born again, you have been given a new nature and a new heart. Saint, you are one with the Lord. You have the same desires as Jesus.

"Grace keeps Christians immature and discourages them from pursuing holiness." Why do we need to pursue that which we already possess? "Because sanctification is progressive," says the holiness preacher. "It's the result of faithful discipline in prayer, Bible study, and purity." But the Bible says holiness is a gift. Like all the blessings of God, holiness comes us to us through grace alone.

> It is because of Him that you are in Christ Jesus, who has become for us wisdom from God — that is, our righteousness, holiness and redemption. (1 Corinthians 1:30)

Do not have any doubts about God's requirements. He requires you to be wholly holy. You're not getting in unless you are. But the hyper-grace gospel declares that the holiness you and I both need is found in Jesus Christ. Sanctification isn't a three-step process, it's a one-step process and Jesus is that step.

"Hyper-grace preachers discourage holy living." Actually, what we discourage is the futile quest to make yourself holy by acting holy. We agree with the New Testament writers who said things like, "You are holy so *be* holy."[28]

Do you see the difference? Under the old covenant it was do-to-become. Act holy and maybe you'll get holy, although no one ever did. But under the new covenant it's do-because-you-are. Be holy because in Christ you *are* holy and you are holy through and through.

How do hyper-grace preachers encourage holiness? Not by getting you to sign up for flesh-powered holiness courses. Instead, our desire is that you will

> Grow in the grace and knowledge of our Lord and Savior Jesus Christ. To Him be glory both now and forever! Amen. (2 Peter 3:18)

There is nothing within us that can save us or sanctify us. Everything we need has to come from above. Everything we need is found in Jesus.

Myth 11: Hyper-grace preachers don't talk about hell and wrath

"Hyper-grace preachers present an unbalanced view of God," say the critics. "They'll tell you about His love but not His wrath or judgment. They'll tell you about heaven but not about hell."

Contrary to what you may have heard, hyper-grace preachers *do* talk about hell, wrath, and judgment. (I have written whole series of articles on these topics and I hardly think I am the only grace-preacher who has done so.) But what we don't do is mix bad news with the good news.

Andrew Wommack writes:

> The gospel is good news — not bad news! That definitely limits what we mean by the word *gospel*.[29]

Those opposed to the modern grace message sometimes claim that we who preach it have left hell out of the gospel. They are correct. Hell is bad news; the gospel is good news. By definition, there can be no bad news in the good news.

Wayne Jacobsen writes that when we use the threat of hell to motivate people to come to God, we are using it in a way Jesus never intended. As a result,

We push people farther away from God's greatest desire rather than inviting them closer to it. His message was not "Come to God or you'll burn in hell." His message was "God's kingdom has come near you and you can become a participant in it."[30]

Jesus was not interested in scaring the hell out of people but inviting all to enter the kingdom of heaven. It's not about what you have been saved from, but what you have been saved to.

It is significant that in his summary of the gospel, Paul never mentions hell:

By this gospel you are saved ... that Christ died for our sins according to the Scriptures, that He was buried, that He was raised on the third day according to the Scriptures.
(1 Corinthians 15:2–4)

Indeed, Paul never mentions hell by name in any of his letters. Although Paul did preach on judgment and the coming wrath he never used the fear of hell to push people into a loving relationship with Jesus. There is no fear in love.

Darrin Hufford writes that we are drawn to God by the Holy Spirit, not threats of hell:

Threats of hell bring fear and condemnation. Only a loveless person could think of such a thing ... God didn't create men to save their souls from hell. He created men and women to have relationships with one another and with Him ... God never delights in people getting what they deserve. He is about saving us from what we deserve.[31]

To place hell at the center of the gospel is to mischaracterize God as a vengeful punisher who sends people to hell, when in truth He is a loving Father who saves His kids from the hell of their own choices.

"Hyper-grace preachers never warn the saints about the coming wrath." Nor does anyone in the Bible. John the Baptist warned the Pharisees and the Sadducees about the coming wrath but you are not a Pharisee or a Sadducee. The gospel is not "be wary of the coming wrath," but "Jesus rescues us from the coming wrath" (see 1 Th. 1:10). For the believer, wrath has been taken out of the equation.

A mixed-grace preacher will blend bad news with good news and insist that the threat of hell is part of the gospel message. He will confuse the saints by telling them God loves them, but if they're not careful they may fall under His judgment and wrath. Those who are saved may become unsaved and those whom God adopts He may yet abandon.

In contrast, a hyper-grace preacher says there's no bad news in the good news. He will seek to woo sinners with the love of God and reassure the saints that no one can snatch them out of their Father's hand. He will say things like "nothing in life or death can separate you from the love of God that is in Christ Jesus" (Rom. 8:38–39).

Myth 12: The hyper-grace gospel makes people lazy

"Grace is a soft gospel for soft Christians," say the critics. "Grace promotes passivity and laziness." It does? Then I guess somebody forgot to tell Paul:

> By the grace of God I am what I am, and His grace to me was not without effect. No, I worked harder than all of them — yet not I, but the grace of God that was with me.
> (1 Corinthians 15:10)

This is not a Grammy speech. This is Paul giving us the secret to his success.

Paul was a tough-as-nails church planter. He wrote letters that would shape the world for 2,000 years. How'd he do it? "I didn't make this happen," said Paul. "God and I did it together."

Grace doesn't make people lazy; it makes them productive and supernaturally fruitful. In contrast with the law that provides no aid to those who trust it, grace makes us soar.

A 300-year-old poem from John Bunyan expresses this perfectly:

Run, John, run, the law commands,
But gives us neither feet nor hands.
Far better news the gospel brings:
It bids us fly and gives us wings.[32]

In his book *Extra Virgin Grace*, Ryan Rufus has a chapter entitled, "More gets done when you rest." This title perfectly captures the relationship between God's grace and our fruitfulness. For as long as you are working *for* the Lord—trying to serve, trying to produce—you cannot bear His fruit. But the moment you start resting in the Lord, He will begin to bear His fruit in you. It's a huge difference.

When I was a pastor, I used to bust my hump in service to the Lord. Any fruit I had was piddling. But since I have learned to rest in God's grace, I have become a thousand times more fruitful. Every grace preacher has the same testimony. Had you heard of Joseph Prince or Andrew Wommack before they started preaching radical grace?

One of the best illustrations of how grace makes us fruitful comes from Tullian Tchividjian's book *One Way Love*. Tchividjian tells the story of two friends who applied for college. One was accepted but the other was deferred. In the subsequent months both friends took similar classes and had a similar workload. But the one who had been accepted into college branched out into a number of extracurricular activities. He started a band, got into rock-climbing, and set up a program for under-privileged kids. The other friend also got involved in extra-curricular activities but he did so in the hope of impressing college acceptance boards. How did things turn out?

At the end of the semester the student who had been deferred was exhausted while the student who had been accepted was full of energy. Free from the pressure to perform and the need to play it safe, the accepted student wrote papers about topics he was genuinely interested in and attained higher grades. Tchividjian concludes that the fruit of assurance was not laziness but creativity, charity, and fun.[33]

The unconditional love of God gives you wings. It inspires you to take risks and be generous with your life. When you are frolicking in the grace of God, work doesn't feel like work. It feels like fun.

"But if you tell people they don't have to do anything for God, they won't." Good! They shouldn't, because your Father is not looking for servants, He's looking for Sons. It's not about what you do for Him. It's about what you and He can do together. By himself the apostle Paul could do nothing, but he and God together changed the world.

"Hyper-grace believers are too lazy to open their Bibles and read Scripture for themselves." Don't fall for the line that says reading a certain number of scriptures or praying a certain length of time impresses God. It doesn't. The New Testament Christians didn't even have Bibles and most of them couldn't read anyway. Yet this did not stop them from walking in their Father's favor and setting the world on fire with the good news of Jesus.[34]

"Grace is irresponsible for it says we have no responsibility to do anything. We have a duty to serve the Lord." In the mouth of a mixed-grace preacher, words like responsibility and duty are the cattle-prods of performance-based Christianity. They convey a sense of obligation that leaves you debt-conscious rather than grace-conscious.

Jesus didn't suffer and die to put you in His debt. He did it to show you how much He loves you. The idea that you are obliged to repay Him for His priceless sacrifice is ludicrous. What can you give Him in consideration for His grace? There is nothing. The instant you give Him anything, it ceases to be grace. Your only "duty" is to say, "Thank you, Jesus!"

In a mixed-grace environment you will feel the pressure to perform and live up to the expectations of others. But walk under pure grace and you find there is no pressure, only the freedom to be who God made you to be. Manmade religion will tell you that you have a responsibility to deliver results for the Lord, but your only responsibility is to shine as a dearly-loved child of God.

We have looked at twelve myths or misperceptions that some have about the hyper-grace gospel. Since I preach this gospel, this list was easy to make. I encounter these misperceptions all the time. Perhaps you have encountered some of them as well.

These twelve myths are pervasive. They regularly appear in articles and books attacking the modern grace message. Every single myth listed here appears in some form in Dr. Brown's book, as we shall discover in Part C.

PART C: A Response to Michael L. Brown

Michael L. Brown's book, *Hyper-Grace: Exposing the Dangers of the Modern Grace Message,* is arguably the best researched and most articulate critique of the modern grace message. The book is 304 pages long, has 15 chapters addressing what Dr. Brown perceives to be the errors in the hyper-grace gospel, and is backed up by more than 30 pages of detailed notes.

Those of us who preach the hyper-grace gospel welcome the discussion and debate that Dr. Brown's book has triggered. We are also grateful for the opportunity to clarify the distinguishing characteristics of this gospel, while also addressing some of the misperceptions surrounding it.

We would encourage everyone who hears our sermons and reads our books to search the Scriptures and ask the Holy Spirit to reveal that which is good and life-giving about our message. As we saw in Part B, much of the beauty of the hyper-grace gospel has been obscured by mischaracterizations and misunderstandings. Dr. Brown is not unaffected by this. Although he identifies some very real points of difference between his message and ours, he also spends considerable effort critiquing things we have never said.

For instance, on page 37 of his book, Dr. Brown identifies four statements that he embraces and we, apparently, reject. They are (1) sanctification is progressive, (2) it's healthy to confess our sins to God, (3) New Testament repentance includes turning away from sins, and (4) the words of Jesus are authoritative. To three of these claims, most hyper-grace preachers would shout amen! Confession is healthy, repentance is often evidenced by a turning away from sins, and everything Jesus said is good and authoritative. The only claim we would reject out of hand is the first one, that sanctification is a process. (More on this below.)

From this passage, which comes early in his book, we can see that a substantial proportion of what Dr. Brown attacks is a mischaracterization of what we are actually saying.

Still, in other places, Dr. Brown is spot on in his summary of our message. He says we claim that God has forgiven all our sins — past, present, future — and we do. He says we are opposed to sin, and we are. And he says we never tell believers that the Holy Spirit convicts them of sin, and we don't.

Like most opponents of the modern grace message, Dr. Brown has an incomplete understanding of what he is opposing. He has it exactly right in some parts, and exactly wrong in others. And this is fine, because we're all learning here. None of us has it all figured out except Jesus.

But while we are not in the business of passing judgment on one other, it is important to recognize the differences in our gospels, because what you do and who you become is influenced by what you believe. To paraphrase Tozer, what you believe about God is just about the most important thing about you. If the message you're hearing paints a mixed-up and confused picture of God, you'll become a mixed-up and confused believer.

As we have seen, the hyper-grace gospel declares that all of God's blessings come to us through grace alone, but a mixed-grace gospel says at least some of His blessings come through our works or performance or obedience. To identify a mixed-grace message, we only need to look for carrots and sticks.

Does Dr. Brown's book offer carrots as a reward for good performance? Indeed, it does. We are told that we will be rewarded with forgiveness if we confess our sins daily (chapter 5) and if our repentance is accompanied by deep sorrow and regret (chapter 6). We are also told that we will be recognized as God's holy children provided that we act holy (chapter 7) and pursue a lifestyle of obedience to New Testament commands (chapters 8 and 12).

And does this book threaten sticks for bad performance? It does that too. We are told that if we sin we displease the Lord (chapter 8) and if we fail to deal quickly with our sin we will no longer enjoy His fellowship (chapter 14). In other words, your relationship with the Lord is only as good as your behavior. If you do well, you can expect His favor. But if you stumble, you should expect His displeasure.

This is frightening stuff but it's only the tip of the iceberg. Read the book carefully, and you will find veiled threats and hints of more serious sanctions. For instance, in chapter 8 Dr. Brown suggests you can get sick and die if you take communion without examining yourself for sin. Although he says in some places that you won't lose your salvation if you don't do the things he prescribes (e.g., on page 59), in other places he says you will. He speaks of believers becoming enemies of God (page 79), hints that if the Jews can be cut off you can too (page 152), and on three occasions says the terrifying warnings of Hebrews 10:26–29 apply to Christians (pages 45, 46 and 105). And then on the last page of his book he suggests that if you don't fly straight but walk away from the Lord you'll forfeit your salvation (page 251).

The implication is clear; if you don't keep the rules and do what you're told, you're toast!

Dr. Brown would no doubt see things differently. He would argue that he is preaching the true gospel while we're the ones sabotaging it with "destructive error" (page 15). According to him and other opponents of the hyper-grace gospel, it's our message of total reliance on our Father's grace that destroys people.[1]

I disagree. What destroys people is the twisted image of a fault-finding, rebuking God who says "be very careful how you live," then makes you sorry when you sin and unchilds you if you don't get back in line. What destroys people—and marriages, families, and churches—are unattainable demands for holy living and threats that Jesus may deny those He has embraced.

It seems clear to me that Dr. Brown advocates performance-based Christianity and uses a mixture of rewards and threats to compel proper behavior. This works-glorifying message is evident in calls for "bloody sweat" and "effort-filled responses" and in appeals to emulate men who were known for their godly resolve and discipline.

Hyper-Grace: Exposing the Dangers of the Modern Grace Message is ostensibly an attack on the hyper-grace gospel, but in reality it is a scary advertisement for the mixed-grace gospel. It trumpets the horrific message that while grace gets you into the kingdom, hard work is required to keep you there. This book may appeal to your sense of religious obligation and duty, but since it puts price-tags on the manifold blessings of God, it has little to do with grace.

But one thing Dr. Brown and I agree on is this: The stakes are huge. Lives are hanging in the balance. Those opposed to the hyper-grace message worry that we who preach it are sending people to hell, while those of us opposed to the mixed-grace message agonize over religious practices that restrict or deny access to God's life-saving grace.

What follows is my chapter-by-chapter response to Dr. Brown's book *Hyper-Grace*. The page numbers below refer to page numbers in the paperback version of the book that was released by Charisma House in January 2014.[2]

Preface

On the first page of his book, Dr. Brown offers two definitions of grace: (1) Grace is God's Riches At Christ's Expense, and (2) it is also "His ongoing empowerment." These are good definitions but a word on empowerment may be in order.

As Joseph Prince has warned:

> Those who teach that grace means "empowerment," they tend to skew it toward a man's works and man's performance. That's not true grace. Remember that divine empowerment comes from Jesus, not you.[3]

Defining grace as empowerment can lead to ungracious conclusions. "Grace helps you obey the Lord," says the preacher of works. "You'd better obey if you want to walk in His grace."

But grace isn't fuel or a lubricant for greasing the cogs of self-effort. It's not about what you do for God at all, but what He has done for you.

What is grace? In a word, grace is *Jesus*. Grace is the divine and undeserved favor of God revealed to us through His Son. If we are living empowered, victorious lives, it is not because of our resolve or hard work. It is because we are trusting in the One who lives in us and through us (see Gal. 2:20).

Chapter 1: Why I love the message of grace

In the opening chapter of his book, Dr. Brown tells an amazing story about the love and grace of his father. When he was a young drug addict, Dr. Brown stole some money from his dad. He cut through a screen door to make it look like an outside job and pointed an accusing finger at his friends. When he later confessed his crime, his father said, "Michael, when I saw the money missing I knew immediately that you had stolen it, and I forgave you on the spot" (page 3).

I love this story for it gives us a picture of our heavenly Father's radical grace and unconditional forgiveness. Note that Michael was forgiven *in his sin*, before he repented, and before he confessed. His father's grace reminds me of Jesus who died for us and carried our sins away "while we were sinners" (Rom. 5:8). It's true that Michael did not experience that forgiveness until he confessed, but the fact was grace had been given. It was there to be received. Michael did nothing to earn it.

This is exactly the sort of unconditional forgiveness that is revealed in the hyper-grace gospel. But it is unlike the forgiveness that Dr. Brown describes later in chapters 4 and 5. How ironic, then, that he should begin a book attacking the hyper-grace gospel with such a hyper-grace story.

Chapter 2: Is there a new grace reformation?

A man once asked me this question: "I want to show my friends that the gospel of grace is not just the latest fad. Can you direct me to some early church teachings on grace?" I replied, "How about the New Testament? Much of what I know about grace comes straight from the life of Jesus and the teachings of the apostles."

The hyper-grace gospel is no new revelation; it's a 2,000-year-old revelation. If you have met Jesus then you have heard the hyper-grace gospel. The problem is you may have heard some other stuff as well – additional material that was never part of the original message. If you're a believer, you don't need to hear the hyper-grace gospel as much as you need to *un*-hear all the extra stuff that obscures the good news of God's grace.

Andrew Farley writes about his journey back to the pure and undiluted gospel in *The Naked Gospel*:

It's amazing how simple and straightforward the naked gospel really is. In fact, most of my exposure to the new (covenant) has involved more *un*learning than learning. Once we remove the clutter from our theological closet, the gospel shines brightly again.[4]

Although the gospel of grace has been around for a long time, in the past few decades technology has helped carry the grace message to places it has never been. Thanks to satellite television and video-sharing websites such as Vimeo and YouTube, sermons proclaiming the hyper-grace gospel are regularly watched by tens of millions of viewers in virtually every country on earth. The spread of this message has also been aided by the proliferation of podcasts, blogs, ebooks, and social media.

One of the neat things about this technological boom is that it has provided platforms to grace-preachers, such as me, who might otherwise have never been heard. As a pulpiteer, I never spoke in stadiums or mega-churches. But as a blogger, I can write an article on grace that will be read by tens of thousands of people within a week.

If past reformations can be linked with a few key individuals, a distinguishing characteristic of the current grace reformation is that no single person or ministry can take the credit. The modern grace message is being proclaimed by hundreds, if not thousands of ordinary people all over the world.

And what is the fruit of this current reformation? Only God knows but I suspect we're talking about many millions of lives being set free from the bondage of DIY religion and the power of sin. All this is to the glory of Jesus whose gospel we preach.

However, in chapter 2 of his book, Dr. Brown shares his view that we are not witnessing a new grace reformation, but the rise of something ugly and destructive. Our message isn't changing the world, it's "lulling many to sleep" (see page 15). I cannot agree with his view that the hyper-grace gospel brings change that is dangerous and ugly, for I've seen too much evidence that it doesn't. As for lulling people to sleep, in my experience grace does the opposite. It revives them to new life. It causes the sinner to awake to righteousness and the saint to rise from the pew of performance-based religion. The grace of God is bearing fruit all over the world.

Page 16: According to hyper-grace teachers it is wrong to ask God to forgive you when you sin. As I said in Part B (see Myth #4), I wouldn't say it's wrong. It's possibly misguided (depending on your motive), but not wrong. There's nothing wrong in asking for grace when you need it. What's wrong is thinking that God won't forgive you unless you ask Him or thinking that God needs your permission before He will forgive you.

Page 17: Dr. Brown repeats an oft-heard claim that hyper-grace preachers preach grace without truth. What is the truth that we neglect to preach? It's holiness. It's God's "requirement" for us to live holy and sin-free lives. Dr. Brown notes with approval a certain deceased Bible teacher who was not just a grace preacher, he was also a holiness preacher. That is "he preached grace and truth" (page 34). Is Dr. Brown correct in saying we hyper-grace preachers are neglecting holiness? We will return to this question when we look at chapter 7 below.

Page 18: A common misperception is that the gospel of grace gives people license to sin. This scandalous claim has been made since the time of Paul and Dr. Brown knows it is a meritless criticism. "Hyper-grace teachers have stated categorically that grace does not give us a license to sin. That is not in question" (page 233). But apparently it *is* in question for he quotes a hyper-grace critic who says this "greasy grace message is once again leading people into sin." By way of illustration, Dr. Brown points to a grace-preaching pastor who is — wait for it — a practicing homosexual. *Aren't you shocked? Aren't you stunned? Can you see now that grace is bad? Gay pastors are preaching this stuff!* In chapter 14 he argues that there is a logical progression between the modern grace message and gay Christians going to nude beaches. In other words, the modern grace message leads inevitably and logically to sin.

Since I have already addressed this misperception in Part B (see Myth #9), I won't respond further here except to say that Dr. Brown's specious reasoning is surprising since it follows this quote from Spurgeon:

If we are to condemn a truth because of the misbehavior of individuals who profess to believe it, we should be found condemning our Lord Himself for what Judas did. (Page 14)

If we are to judge men by the company they keep, then surely we must condemn Jesus, for He was a friend of sinners. It's possible that Jesus was even a friend of gays and lesbians. *Somebody pass the smelling salts!* I am not a homosexual and I don't condone homosexuality. But I will just as happily break bread with the gay pastor as with the religious man who frowns upon him.

Chapter 3: Name-calling, judgmentalism, and divisiveness in the name of grace

Name-calling is an ugly aspect of religious disagreement. For preaching a hyper-grace message I have been called a wolf, a heretic, the antichrist, and more besides. It goes with the territory. But as far as I am aware, no hyper-grace preacher has ever called Dr. Brown a bad name, and why would they? In my brief association with Dr. Brown, he has struck me as the sort of person who would not be bothered by name-calling in any case. So I was surprised to find a chapter addressing these secondary issues in his book.

Page 23: When respected preachers like Clark Whitten and Rob Rufus talk about legalistic people or modern Pharisees, they are being judgmental and divisive, says Dr. Brown. Apparently, one gets the sense that anyone who disagrees with their message is a grace hater and an enemy of the gospel. "Can you see how problematic this kind of rhetoric is?" (page 25). Indeed, I can. Yet I find this hand-wringing over name-calling and judgmentalism a bit rich coming from a man who doesn't hesitate to name names and who has written a judgmental book identifying specific individuals as the authors of destructive errors. Can't Dr. Brown see how problematic *that* is?

Pages 27–9: In any large group of believers you will find a few people saying harsh words about others on social media platforms such as Facebook. What surprises me is that Dr. Brown sees fit to reproduce some of these attacks from the fringe in his book. It's as if he is saying, "Look at the unkind things this person said about me on Facebook. That is the fruit of grace."

If this is an attempt to discredit the grace message, it is not a convincing one. Being criticized is a fact of life for preachers of any stripe. It is ludicrous to conclude from Facebook rants that the message of grace is bankrupt.

A quote which has been attributed to Martin Luther comes to mind:

> Do you suppose that abuses are eliminated by destroying the object which is abused? Men can go wrong with wine and women. Shall we then prohibit and abolish women?

Facebookers can go wrong with grace. Shall we then prohibit grace?

Page 30: I get mentioned for preaching against a counterfeit gospel. Apparently I go too far when I say a counterfeit gospel will make you a target for tyrants and manipulators. Yet in the next paragraph the apostle Paul is mentioned for saying those who preach a counterfeit gospel should be eternally condemned! Surely what's good for one Paul is good for the other. If the apostle Paul doesn't go too far, then neither do I. You might say that by the standard of God's Word, I don't go far enough.

Chapter 4: Has God already forgiven our future sins?

Hyper-grace preachers claim that God has forgiven all our sins. Dr. Brown disagrees. Although Jesus paid for every sin we will ever commit, "the transaction of forgiveness takes place at different points in time" (page 41). On my first reading, I thought Dr. Brown was drawing a line between what God has done (forgiven us) and how we respond to what God has done (receive His forgiveness). If so, I agree there is a gap. God forgave you long ago but if you haven't received His forgiveness, you won't walk in it. Grace has to be believed to be beneficial (see Heb. 4:2).

But Dr. Brown is not saying this at all. Referring to the cross he asks, "Were we forgiven at that point in time? Absolutely not!" Never mind that Jesus went to the cross to carry away your sins; never mind that Christ said of His redemptive work, "it is finished;" and never mind that Paul said God forgave all your sins "when you were dead in your sins" (Col. 2:13). See the difference?

The hyper-grace gospel says you were forgiven; the mixed-grace gospel says you weren't.

The apostle Paul told the Corinthians that God tore down the dividing barrier separating Him from the world and He is no longer "counting men's sins against them" (2 Cor. 5:19). Dr. Brown seems to disagree for he says that until we got saved "our sins *were* still counted against us, separating us from God" (page 41, my italics).

Chad Mansbridge is an author and pastor of a church in South Australia. He writes:

> Much of the debate surrounding the question of whether Christians can or should ask God to forgive their sins, would be quickly resolved once forgiveness is properly defined. Simply put, forgiveness is the cancellation of a debt. If you believe that God keeps a record of your wrongs and holds a sin-debt against you when you disobey or dishonor Him, then of course it makes sense to ask Him for forgiveness. Get your debt cleared as soon as you can! However, I suggest you believe the Holy Spirit's promise that God will never count your sins against you.[5]

Dr. Brown says Jesus *paid* for all your sins but hasn't *forgiven* you for all your sins. This is a strange thing to say. If Jesus has settled the account, then the account is settled. If Jesus has paid the debt, there is no more debt. All your sins were carried away (i.e., forgiven) at the cross.

You may ask, "But what about the sins I haven't committed yet?" Evidently Dr. Brown thinks this an absurd question (see page 42). *What Christian thinks about committing sins? If you think like this, you should take a good look at yourself.* But it's not a ridiculous question if you have been taught that you are only for-given up to a certain point in time. It is a legitimate question and those who preach conditional forgiveness ought to answer it, as Dr. Brown does in chapter 5.

Dr. Brown notes that there is not one verse in the Bible that pronounces us already forgiven for our future sins (page 43). Nor is there any verse that says Jesus will come and die a second time for your sins. One goes with the other. The Bible declares Christ died one time to "do away with sin" (Heb. 9:26). Either His one-time sacrifice was a sufficient remedy for all your sins — past, present, future — or it wasn't. If it was, open your mouth and thank Him. If it wasn't, fall down in despair because if the Son of God can't deal with your sin, then you have no chance of success. [6]

Dr. Brown quotes Acts 3:19 where Peter exhorts his Jewish hearers to repent and turn to God "for your sins being blotted out" (Young's Literal Translation). Dr. Brown says Peter is only referring to their *past* sins. In other words, only *some* of your sins have been blotted out or carried away. But why limit Christ's propitiation in this way?

This is how I read Peter's words:

> Repent — *change your unbelieving mind* — and turn back to God — *from whom we have all run away* — for your sins — *all of them, every last one* — being — *have been and now in fact are* — blotted out. *And as you receive, through faith, His gracious gift of forgiveness* — times of refreshing shall come from the Lord — *which is surely good news since you are probably cut to the heart like the Jews I preached to the other day were when I said they crucified the Messiah.* (Acts 3:19, my paraphrase)

Elsewhere in his book, Dr. Brown talks about how the blood of Jesus purchased "complete redemption and forgiveness for us, providing the complete and total payment of every one of our sins" (page 115). To this I shout a hearty amen! *Complete* is the critical word. Everything that needed to be done to set you free was completed at the cross.

But if Dr. Brown speaks of *complete* redemption in chapter 8, how then can he speak of *incomplete* forgiveness in chapter 4? How does he reconcile this inconsistency?

He does it by describing Christ's sacrifice as a million-dollar deposit made on a debit card (see page 43). This is how it works. If you sinned this morning you are not forgiven until you repent and draw upon that cross-wrought provision. In other words, between the time you sin and the time you repent, you are an unforgiven child of God. I find this illustration is at odds with Scripture since the New Testament epistle writers nowhere describe the saints as unforgiven. Nor do they exhort us to ask God for forgiveness.

Dr. Brown's debit card illustration is also at odds with his own experience as a petty thief. When he sinned his father forgave him on the spot, *before* he repented and confessed. True, Dr. Brown did not know he was forgiven but his ignorance did not change the fact that he was. Similarly, our ignorance has no bearing on the finished work of the cross except to stop us from enjoying the benefits of what Christ has accomplished.

The debit card metaphor is an unbiblical, grace-killing picture that promotes performance-based Christianity. It suggests that when we come to Christ, our sin debt is paid off but, and there is always a *but* in the mixed-grace message, every time we sin we incur a fresh debt which will be held to our account until we take steps to fix it. How is this not mixing grace with works?

It is essential that you settle this issue of forgiveness in your heart, for if you don't you risk setting aside grace in the pursuit of what God has already given you. The hyper-grace gospel declares that you have been completely forgiven on account of Jesus. Do you believe this? Here's a simple test to find out. Just ask yourself whether you agree with this Psalm of David's:

> Praise the Lord, my soul, and forget not all His benefits — who forgives all your sins ... (Psalm 103:2–3a)

All means *all*. All does not mean only those sins you have specifically repented of and confessed. During His time on earth, Jesus forgave plenty of people who had done neither.

> For as high as the heavens are above the earth, so great is His love for those who fear Him; as far as the east is from the west, so far has He removed our transgressions from us.
> (Psalm 103:11–12)

In this Psalm, David links God's unconditional forgiveness with His unconditional love. Do you see? If God's love is unconditional (and it is for there is no other kind), then His forgiveness must be unconditional too. You have been completely and eternally forgiven on account of your Father's great love. This is the hyper-grace gospel!

Page 44: Dr. Brown writes that it would be foolish to argue that Paul saw the sins of believers but God didn't see them. Indeed, it *would* be foolish, which may be why no hyper-grace preacher is saying such a thing. If they were, Dr. Brown would've quoted them in his book.

Does God see our sins? Since God sees everything He must. Our sins grieve Him and make Him sad because He is our Father who loves us dearly. When we hurt ourselves and each other, it hurts Him. No hyper-grace teacher would say otherwise (see Myth #5 in Part B). But because of Jesus, God is not counting our sins against us (2 Cor. 5:19). It's not that God has become senile and absent-minded in regards to sin. But out of love He chooses not to hold our sins against us (Heb. 10:17).

Pages 45–6: Dr. Brown quotes two scriptures from Hebrews to support his idea that God won't forgive you unless you first do something. Naturally, hyper-grace preachers disagree with this works-based interpretation. You were forgiven at the cross. But if all your sins have been carried away, why are there scriptures in the New Testament warning us about the dangers of sin? They are not there to make you doubt God's grace. They are there because the consequences of sin are many and varied. Sin can hurt you, make you sick, and grieve the Holy Spirit. But the one thing sin cannot do, is undo the finished work of the cross and cause God to un-forgive you. No matter how great your sin, His grace is greater still (Rom. 5:20).

Page 47: Dr. Brown wonders why Jesus exposes the sins of His people, as He does in Revelation 2–3? Probably because He loves us and cares for us and doesn't want us to be destroyed by sin. The Revelation letters are significant not just for what they say but also what they don't say. Jesus never says to these guys, "Your sin is greater than my work. You're no longer forgiven. Grace has been taken off the table."[7]

Page 47: Dr. Brown also wonders why James wrote, "Cleanse your hands, you sinners." Dr. Brown uses this passage from James 4:8 to support his view that Christians need to ask for forgiveness. But James' epistle is addressed to a mixed audience of believers and unbelievers, sinners and saints. In this particular passage, James is speaking to sinners, not Christians. As Dr. Brown recognizes elsewhere (on pages 93–4), sinners are not saints and saints are not sinners. Those who have been washed by Jesus don't need to be washed again (John 15:3).

To answer the question — why does James write like this? — it's because sinners need to be cleansed from their sins just as the proud need to humble themselves to receive the grace that God freely gives (Jas. 4:6,10).

Chapter 5: Should believers confess their sins to God?

In many hyper-grace books it is common to find some discussion on 1 John 1:9. This verse is special because it is the only verse in the new covenant that appears to link confession of sins with God's forgiveness. If this verse was in the old covenant it would be no great thing, but because it's in the new it stands out.

Clark Whitten writes:

> Whenever the subjects of sin and the need of confession are raised, this verse is universally quoted and trotted out as a proof text. Why? Because there aren't any others to quote![8]

1 John 1:9 is often used to support a mixed-grace message of conditional forgiveness. "God won't forgive you unless you review all of your sins." Naturally this message is incompatible with grace and everything else the new covenant says about forgiveness.

Dr. Brown is well acquainted with the grace-based interpretation of 1 John 1:9. He's read our books. However, he has two points of contention.

First, who are the "we" John is referring to when he says, "If *we* confess our sins … "?

Some (including me) have said that John is referring to unbelievers. However, Dr. Brown says *we* means *us* (page 57). John is referring to Christians because we all get dirty from time to time and need to be re-cleansed.

Perhaps we don't need to get too worked up over exactly who John had in mind when he wrote this verse. I think we can agree that we all need Jesus to cleanse us from sin and unrighteousness—every single one of us. That's what John is saying here. "If we … He will …"

The real question is whether He will cleanse us from *all* sin or only *some* sin (specifically the sin we confess). Does He cleanse from *all* unrighteousness or only *some* unrighteousness? Here John is unequivocal. Jesus cleanses us from "*all* unrighteousness."

The first chapter of 1 John contains a number of imperatives that should not be confusing to the reader. If you are not walking *in the light* you need to get *in the light*. But if you are *in the light* you don't need to get *in the light* because you already are *in the light*.

Similarly, if you have not been cleansed *from all unrighteousness*, then you need to be cleansed *from all unrighteousness*. But if you have been cleansed *from all unrighteousness*, then you don't need to be cleansed *from all unrighteousness* because you already have been cleansed *from all unrighteousness*.

I'm sorry to labor this point, but it seems John's words are confusing to some people.

Here's the second point of contention: What exactly is confession?

As we saw in Part B, confession, as John uses the term, does not mean reviewing your sins. It means "to say the same thing as another" or "to agree with" God (see Myth #2). In this case we are agreeing that we have sinned and are in need of cleansing.

So far so good. Yet Dr. Brown further notes that the Greek word for confess speaks of continuous action as opposed to a one-time act (page 58).

Why does John say we need to keep confessing? Remember, confessing means agreeing with God. It's the definition of faith and the native language of a believer.

In context, confession means agreeing with what God says about our sins. It means that if I sin and act unfaithfully I agree with God that He remains faithful and has cleansed me from *all* unrighteousness including the unrighteous thing I just did. I agree that Christ alone is the cure for my failings and that anything I do to atone for my sin will only tarnish the sublime perfections of His redemptive work.

Contrary to the recommendations of DIY religion, I don't need to speak to God about my sins because Jesus speaks for me (1 John 2:1).

Dr. Brown has a different understanding. According to him, continually confessing means continually reviewing your sins for the purposes of being forgiven. When you got saved you were forgiven. Then you sinned and became unforgiven. In the heavenly accounts your name was scratched out of the forgiven column and entered into the unforgiven column where it will remain until you confess. This is called conditional forgiveness and it is preached nowhere in the new covenant.

The idea that God withholds His forgiveness until we confess creates an intriguing problem for the mixed-grace preacher, for didn't Jesus say harboring unforgiveness is a sin? If we don't confess and God doesn't forgive, doesn't that mean God is guilty of breaking His own commands?

Dr. Brown wriggles out of this by inventing different levels of forgiveness. There's the forgiveness of salvation, which is never withdrawn, and then there is the less secure forgiveness of friendship which sometimes is (page 59). Apparently, God harbors only the second and lesser kind of unforgiveness, which I guess means He's only a lesser sinner and not a great one like the saint who needs to confess.

Page 59: Dr. Brown stresses that when we sin we do not need to get saved all over again. When you sin you are still saved; you're just not forgiven. Forgive me for running off on a tangent here, but the suggestion that Christians are not forgiven unless they specifically confess each sin intrigues me. Since it is impossible to confess all our sins, especially the numerous sins of omission, do we conclude that the church is full of unforgiven Christians?

"Paul, you're being pedantic. Of course you don't need to confess *all* your sins. You only need to confess the ones you did on purpose." So you're saying God turns a blind eye to some of our sin? Because I thought sin was sin.

No matter how well you dress her, confessing-to-be-forgiven is the bone-ugly love-child of dead religion and the universal but faithless desire for self-improvement. Her mouth is full of lies for she would have you believe that the church is made up of unforgiven Christians worshipping an unforgiving God. If you've been dating this hideous hag, it's time to end the relationship.

But I digress.

Page 60: Dr. Brown maintains that we do not confess sins to get re-saved but to restore our fractured relationship with God. Apparently this is what Jesus had in mind when He taught us to daily pray, "Forgive us our debts." Actually, Jesus taught us to ask for daily *bread* not daily forgiveness. Asking for forgiveness on a daily basis seems silly to me. What if we miss a day? What if we haven't sinned? Can you imagine some of the conversations we might have with God?

"Lord, forgive me."

"Why, what did you do?"

"I don't know. This is just a general-purpose confession. Why not put this one in the tank for next time?"

It would be funny except there are people out there who actually live like this. It breaks my heart. These dear folk are bound with guilt and are constantly fretting about the sins they need to confess. They need to hear the good news of God's complete and unconditional forgiveness.

Page 60: I get mentioned as having "a real problem" with conditional forgiveness. Indeed, I do. If I trained my children to ask me for forgiveness on a daily basis, even when they had done nothing wrong, I would be an abnormal father. And if they sinned and I withheld my forgiveness *until* they repented and confessed, I would be an unloving father. I would certainly be less of a dad than Dr. Brown's father.

I don't know if Dr. Brown's dad was a Christian when he forgave his son but he sure acted like one:

Bear with each other and forgive one another if any of you has a grievance against someone. Forgive as the Lord forgave you. (Colossians 3:13)

We are not supposed to wait until those who sin against us repent and confess before we forgive them. We're supposed to forgive them *as the Lord forgave us.* On the cross Jesus forgave the men who put Him there (Luke 23:34). These were men who hated Him, cursed Him, and tortured Him. None of these men confessed or repented. Some of them actually thought they were doing the Lord's work. Yet Jesus forgave them all.

This is how it is supposed to be with us. We are to forgive *as the Lord forgave us*. If we waited for everyone who hurt us to apologize and 'fess up before we forgave them we would become embittered grace-killers (see Heb. 12:15).

Does this mean hyper-grace preachers are opposed to confession of sin? Of course not. We are merely saying there is a difference between healthy and unhealthy confession. Healthy confession, or agreeing with God, helps us receive grace and is useful for breaking the power of sin in our lives. But unhealthy confession, which is verbalizing unbelief in the goodness of God and the finished work of the cross, perpetuates a cycle of Adamic self-reliance and death.[9]

Page 63: Dr. Brown disputes the hyper-grace teaching that says "the moment you were saved, your future sins were pronounced forgiven." Well if we're defining forgiveness as the Bible does (literally, the carrying away of sins), then you'd better hope this is true because Jesus isn't going back to the cross. Incidentally, we don't say your sins were forgiven the moment you were saved. You were forgiven much earlier than that.

Pages 66–7: Dr. Brown quotes at length from an article attacking the "imbecilic, ignorant, or crazy" logic that says there is no need for Christians to repent or otherwise deal with "momentary blemishes and spots." Since I don't know any hyper-grace preacher who says such imbecilic, ignorant, and crazy things, I see no need to respond. For more on the myth that hyper-grace preachers are against repentance, see Part B (Myth #1).

Chapter 6: The Holy Spirit, conviction of sin, and repentance

Just as there is only one verse in the New Testament linking confession with forgiveness, there is only one verse linking the Holy Spirit's conviction with sin (John 16:8). But what a mountain has been built on that one verse! Here are three points of view:

(1) Dr. Brown says the Holy Spirit convicts Christians of their sins
(2) Most grace preachers say the Holy Spirit never convicts Christians of their sins
(3) Some grace preachers also say the Holy Spirit never convicts anyone – saved or unsaved – of their sins

(If you're wondering how the third viewpoint could possibly be Biblical, it's based on the stunning revelation that Christ did away with all our sin on the cross and there is nothing left to convict. The Holy Spirit seeks to convict or convince sinners of that truth. "Regarding sin, see Jesus. Trust Him.")

Page 73: Most hyper-grace preachers agree that the Holy Spirit never convicts believers of their sin. However, Dr. Brown says that the Holy Spirit, as an expression of His love and kindness, "makes us uncomfortable in our sins." He notes that the Greek word for convict can mean several things but mainly suggests fault-finding and rebuke (see pages 75–6). But if it's the Holy Spirit's practice to find fault and rebuking us, why did He inspire Paul to write 1 Corinthians 13:5? Perhaps Paul misheard because apparently love *does* find fault and keep a record of wrongs.

Page 74: The Holy Spirit says to the believer, "You have sinned." Really? Why would the Spirit of Christ seek to remind you of the sins Christ has carried away? It's like Jesus removed your sins as far as the east is from the west but His Spirit went on a looooong trip and brought them back again. It's as though the blood of the Lamb blotted out all your sins (Is. 43:25), but the Holy Spirit wrote them back in again. It's like God the Father is sitting on the throne of grace saying, "In honor of Jesus I choose to forget your sins," but the Holy Spirit is saying, "Don't worry Lord, I'll help you remember them." It's ridiculous.

How exactly does the Holy Spirit convict us? Through the law, says Dr Brown on page 77. "It is by God's law that we are convicted – the very Law that hyper-grace teachers want to throw under the bus as dangerous and destructive." And the very law that the hyper-grace preacher Paul said ministered death and condemnation (2 Cor. 3:7–9). Put this altogether and you discover that the Spirit of Life is really a Minister of Death and your loving Father, who said He keeps no record of wrongs, actually does keep a record of wrongs. Something doesn't add up.

(Incidentally, why does Law get a capital "L" throughout Dr. Brown's book, while grace must get by with a little "g"? Is Dr. Brown trying to tell us something about the relative unimportance of grace with respect to the Law?)

Page 77: Dr. Brown writes that he has been convicted of sin many times while reading the law and that each time this has caused him to run to God and fall at His feet. His experience testifies to the true ministry of the law—it helps us recognize sin and our need for grace. But the law is not the Holy Spirit and the Spirit of Grace does not minister to you through the law.

Look into the mirror of the law and you will always feel condemned (2 Cor. 3:9). This may explain why Dr. Brown defines conviction (*elegcho*) as fault-finding and rebuke (see page 75). But an interpretation of *elegcho‾*which is more consistent with the Holy Spirit's gracious character may be *expose*, or *bring into the light*. How does the Holy Spirit convict us? He does it by turning on the lights, not to shame you (Jesus carried your shame), but to show you the way to life. Ian Thomas describes it like this:

> The Holy Spirit is like a man with a lamp entering a dark and dirty room, and what you have learned to live with in the dark becomes repugnant in the light.[10]

Think of Saul on the road to Damascus (Acts 9:3). By his own account he was chief of sinners. Then the lights went on and he became a different man.

I have written elsewhere about the need for a new covenant definition of conviction, one that does not emphasize your badness but God's goodness and grace.

> The Holy Spirit's conviction has nothing to do with your sin and everything to do with God's grace. It's not about the bad thing you've done but the good thing He wants to do in you right now.[11]

Pages 79–90: What is godly sorrow? Apparently it's when the Holy Spirit makes you sorry for your sin. *God grieves over you, you sorry excuse for a Christian. You have become an enemy of God!* Or perhaps the godly sorrow that Paul refers to is the sorrow the Corinthians felt when they read his letter. Maybe it's the sorrow we all experience when we realize we have made a hash of things and grieved our Father.

Is there pain and discomfort involved with conviction? Often there is. But this pain is not inflicted by the Holy Spirit. It is the regret of realizing we have missed the mark. Do you think Saul was happy to learn he had been persecuting the Lord?

Our hearts vibrate in harmony with God's. We sing the songs of love together. But when we sin we sing out of key. This dissonance affects our heart – it causes discomfort and makes us want to get back in tune. The problem is we've lost our place in the song. We can't find the right note. But the Spirit of Grace helps us. He sings in our ear, on key, and we pick up the tune again.[12]

Beginning on page 82, Dr. Brown quotes some grace teachers who say repentance is defined as a change of mind, an about-face. This is not good enough, says Dr. Brown. A change of mind without an accompanying change of action is worthless. I don't know anyone who would disagree with him. But any action will be the fruit of repentance and not repentance itself.

What sort of behavior does Dr. Brown expect to see before determining whether your repentance is sufficient? Since repentance is the result of a Holy Spirit's fault-finding and rebuke, he anticipates it will include sorrow and grief (page 84). True repentance, apparently, is marked by regret, tears, and grief-stricken anguish.

Spurgeon had a different view:

A curious idea men have of what repentance is! Many fancy that so many tears are to be shed, and so many groans are to be heaved, and so much despair is to be endured. Whence comes this unreasonable notion? Unbelief and despair are sins, and therefore I do not see how they can be constituent elements of acceptable repentance; yet there are many who regard them as necessary parts of true Christian experience.

They are in great error ... To repent is to change your mind
about sin, and Christ, and all the great things of God.[13]

An appeal for an emotional response possibly makes sense if you
define repentance as turning from sin. *Look at that filthy, yucky
thing you did! Quick, turn away!* But repentance is bigger than that.
Every time I learn something from the Bible and change my mind,
that's repentance. Every time the Holy Spirit reveals something
awesome about the character of God that I did not properly
understand, that's repentance too. My mind is renewed, it's
changed, and this change will be reflected in the way I act. I repent
every day and typically do so with great joy rather than sorrow
and grief.

Page 82: Dr. Brown tells the tale of the prodigal son to
illustrate repentance. He observes that the prodigal recognized the
folly of his ways and became eager to confess and get right with
his father. Indeed, the prodigal *was* a fool for trading the life of a
prince for the life of a pig. Sitting in the muck and swill it
would've been hard not to recognize the folly of his ways. Similarly, when we make dumb choices we'll feel foolish too. There's
nothing supernatural or surprising about this. The real surprise in
the story is how the father reacts to his son's stupidity.

Does the father convict the son of his sin? No. Does the father
find fault, rebuke, or shame the son? No. Does the father inflict
sorrow on the son? No. Does the father hear the son's confession?
No. He cuts the son off mid-speech. Then, and most surprisingly
of all, the father starts organizing a party. Do you see? Jesus'
amazing story refutes everything Dr. Brown says about the Holy
Spirit's conviction and your need to feel sorrowful and unworthy.

This reminds me of something Andrew Wommack has said:

If you feel like you're so sorry, then praise Him for the fact
that He loves such a sorry person as you! Instead of focusing
on your unworthiness, thank Him for His goodness.[14]

Page 90: Several years ago I created a bit of a stir when I published
an article entitled "Three reasons why I don't preach repentance
(turn from sin)." (Yes, I now appreciate that a title like that was

going to mark me as someone who is opposed to repentance, even though I said at the time that "there needs to be far more repentance, particularly from believers.")[15]

In the article I wrote that "repentance in the old covenant meant turning from sin but repentance in the new means turning to God." On the contrary, says Dr. Brown. Repentance means turning away from sin and turning to God. I'm not sure if Dr. Brown is confused or being disingenuous here so let me briefly restate my original point.

Turning from sin makes you neither righteous nor holy. An unbeliever who turns from sin remains an unbeliever. Consider the Pharisees. They ran away anytime sin appeared — they were moral people — yet Jesus called them sons of hell (Matt. 23:15).

As the Pharisees demonstrated on a daily basis, you can turn from sin without turning to God. So telling people to turn from sin won't necessarily lead them any place good, which is why I don't do it.

Perhaps Dr. Brown understands this but feels I am giving insufficient air-time to sin. To this I plead "guilty as charged." In all things I aspire to be Christ-conscious rather than sin-conscious. I am not minimizing sin and its destructive effects. I am glorifying Jesus and His gracious benefits. I see no reason why we should spend half the time preaching "turn from sin" and half the time preaching "turn to Jesus". I'd rather just preach Jesus.

Repentance *for* the forgiveness of sins is an old covenant concept. It's doing (repenting) to get (forgiveness). It's tit for tat and *quid pro quo*. Such thinking has nothing to do with grace. Repentance in the new covenant is a reaction to what God has done. It's the change of heart Zacchaeus experienced after he encountered the Lord of grace.

In a related note (see Dr. Brown's endnote 53 on page 262), I am mentioned for saying that the word Jesus uses for forgiveness in Luke 24:47 is a noun (a thing), rather than a verb (an action). Dr. Brown disputes this and lists a few scriptures to prove that God's forgiveness is not the noun Jesus said it was. I'm always puzzled when someone says I'm wrong right after I have quoted Jesus word for word, and I am surprised that a scholar such as Dr. Brown would seek to challenge such an easily-proved point. Anyone with access to a Greek lexicon can determine whether Jesus was using verbs or nouns in Luke 24:47. But to save you the trouble, and to clarify the point I was originally trying to make, here are all the New Testament mentions of divine forgiveness expressed as a verb (*aphiemi*) and a noun (*aphesis*):

	Before the Cross	After the Cross
Aphiemi (verb) G863	Matt. 6:12,14,15, 9:2,5,6 12:31,32 18:27,32,35, Mark 2:5,7,9,10, 3:28, 4:12, 11:25,26, Luke 5:20,21,23,24, 7:47,48,49, 11:4, 12:10, 23:34	Acts 8:22, Rom. 4:7, Jas 5:15, I John 1:9, 2:12
Aphesis (noun) G859	Matt. 26:28, Mark 1:4, 3:29, Luke 1:77, 3:3 4:18	Luke 24:47, Acts 2:38, 5:31, 10:43, 13:38, 26:18, Eph. 1:7, Col 1:14, Heb. 9:22, 10:18

From this little scripture study we can draw one extraordinary conclusion: the cross changed the meaning of the word forgiveness.

Before the cross, divine forgiveness was mainly described as a verb to be done (*aphiemi*); but after the cross, it was typically described as a noun to be received (*aphesis*). Before the cross, God's forgiveness was never expressed as a noun (except when used in a prophetic foretelling of new covenant forgiveness); after the cross it was rarely described as a verb (except when there were good reasons for doing so, such as quoting the Old Testament).

This distinction becomes even more obvious when we focus on the words of Jesus. Before the cross Jesus described forgiveness as a verb and never as a noun (except when looking ahead to the new covenant). After the cross Jesus described forgiveness as a noun and never as a verb.

Do you see? The cross of Calvary changed the message. Prior to the cross, forgiveness was something *God does*, but after the cross forgiveness became something *God's done*.

It seems to me that if Jesus preached and demonstrated unconditional forgiveness, so should we. As Peter (Acts 2:38, 5:31) and then Paul (Acts 10:43, 13:38) said on several occasions, forgiveness is a gift to be received and not a wage to be earned. We are not forgiven in accordance with our acts of confession or contrition but in accordance with the riches of God's grace.

Chapter 7: Sanctified or not?

The hyper-grace gospel declares that when you were born again and joined to the Lord, you became just as righteous and holy as He is. Dr. Brown sort of agrees but he also advocates progressive sanctification. "I agree with modern grace teachers when they state that we have already been sanctified, but that is only part of the story. The Word plainly states that we are being sanctified" (page 98).

So are you holy or not? The answer, apparently, is yes and no. You are, but you aren't. (I know, it doesn't make any sense to me either.)

Progressive sanctification is the old carrot that says you're holy but you're not really, so act holy then one day, maybe, you'll become holy. This idea is based on scriptures such as Hebrews 10:14 (ESV) which say "He has perfected for all time those *who are being sanctified.*" However, other Bibles translate this passage differently. For instance, the King James Version says, "For by one offering He hath perfected for ever *them that are sanctified.*" Do you see the difference? One Bible says you are sanctified, the other says you are being sanctified. Big difference.

No matter which translation you read, Hebrews 10:14 also says, "He has perfected us," and the verb here is *teleioō* which means "to complete." This is good news for imperfect, incomplete man: Jesus completes us.[16]

Except that He doesn't, apparently, because progressive sanctification says you are a work in progress. You're an incomplete, partial saint. So pull your socks up and act holy and maybe you'll become a full saint and a complete Christian. This sort of logic appeals to our desire for self-improvement, but it isn't Biblical:

And you are complete in Him ... (Colossians 2:10a, NKJV)

He who has Christ lacks no good thing. In Him you are fully, completely, and totally sanctified.

Dr. Brown reads Paul's epistles as though they were handbooks for progressive sanctification. He writes of Paul's demand for a lifestyle that requires effort and obedience (page 99). The words *demand* and *require* should raise red flags. In what sense is holy living demanded and required? And what happens if you fail to live up to these demands and requirements?

Dr. Brown doesn't come right out and say it but he quotes someone who says the goal of sanctification is eternal life. Put one and one together and you'll get two. If you don't deliver on the required performance — if you fail to do all the things listed in the New Testament and attain the requisite level of holiness — you won't inherit eternal life. How is this not a message of works-based salvation?

Under the old covenant holiness was demanded of unholy men. But under the new covenant, holiness is freely given to unholy men through Jesus Christ (see 1 Cor. 1:30).

Holiness preaching that emphasizes *what you must do* is carnal Christianity. Make no mistake, it comes straight out of the old covenant. Heed this sort of teaching and you will exalt the flesh at the expense of grace. And it won't make you holy.

On page 96 Dr. Brown quotes a theologian who says our past holiness is merely *positional* (i.e., not real) while our current holiness is progressive (i.e., as good as you make it). To paraphrase Bill Gillham, that's like saying God is deceiving Himself by only pretending we're holy when we're actually grubby.[17]

So are you sanctified or not? What is the answer to the question that is the title of this chapter? This is what the gospel declares:

> You were washed, *you were sanctified*, you were justified in the name of the Lord Jesus Christ and by the Spirit of our God.
> (1 Corinthians 6:11b, my italics)

You *were* sanctified by the Spirit of God. You are not sanctified through any effort of your own. Your personal pursuit of holiness didn't aid God one bit.

> Do you not know that you are God's temple and that God's Spirit dwells in you? ... For God's temple is holy, and you are that temple. (1 Corinthians 3:16–17, ESV)

A Christian is someone who has been joined to the Lord and has received the Holy Spirit as a deposit guaranteeing what is to come (2 Cor. 5:5). Do you think the Holy Spirit lives in an unholy temple? To quote Ralph Harris, you are God's sacred mobile home. "He didn't make you just a believer. He made you an excellent place in which to live."[18]

You may say, "But I don't *feel* holy." Your sanctification is not something to feel, it's something to believe. It's a faith thing. God has done His part. Your part is to say, "Yes Lord, I trust what you say. I am the holy temple of your Holy Spirit."

> Therefore, I urge you, brothers and sisters, in view of God's mercy, to offer your bodies as a living sacrifice, holy and pleasing to God — this is your true and proper worship.
> (Romans 12:1)

We are exhorted to present our bodies as living and holy sacrifices to the Lord. Is your body living? Then your body is holy. (So much for the idea that only the spiritual part of you is holy.)

You may ask, "If we are already holy, then why does God call us to be holy?" He's calling us to be who we truly are. He is saying, "You are my sanctified children. Act like it. Be who I made you to be."

As D. Martyn Lloyd-Jones once said:

> Holiness is not something we are called upon to do in order that we may become something; it is something we are to do because of what we already are ...[19]

"Paul, I'm still confused. It seems there are a lot of scriptures exhorting us to become holy. How do we reconcile those with other scriptures that say that we are already holy?" The best answer I've heard comes from Bill Gillham, who compares Christians to oak trees:

> Are Christians a truly holy people, or are we trying to *become* a holy people? ... As an oak sapling grows, it doesn't get

"oakier." Oak is oak. It simply *matures into* what it is, a full-grown oak tree.[20]

You don't become an oak tree by acting like an oak tree; nor do you become holy by acting holy. Jesus makes you holy. Your part is to mature into what He has already made you. This takes time, but just as a baby never becomes more human as it grows, you will never become more holy as you mature. You simply grow into who God has already made you to be.

> Needless to say, maturity doesn't occur in one giant leap, but through a process: "But we all … are being transformed into the same image from glory to glory" (2 Corinthians 3:18). Notice it's "from glory to glory," not "from garbage to glory." You are already holy in Christ … Just as an oak sapling does not get *oakier* as it matures, neither does a new creature in Christ get holier, more forgiven, more accepted, etc.[21]

Critics of the modern grace message say we who preach it are opposed to holy living. As we saw in Part B, nothing could be further from the truth (see Myth #10). What we are opposed to is the old habit of trying to make yourself holy by acting holy. You just can't do it. The standard is too high. But the good news declares God makes us holy. He takes the shards of our broken lives and makes something beautiful, pleasing, sweet-smelling, and Christ-like.

New Testament exhortations to live holy should not be read as a self-help guide to holiness. Rather, they are pictures of the wholesome, healthy life we get to enjoy as we allow Christ to express His holy life through us. They are advertisements for the abundant life that is already ours in Christ.

Now that we have a good understanding of why the Bible calls us to be holy, we can look at some of the scriptures Dr. Brown cites in this chapter:

> To all those in Rome who are loved by God and called to be saints (Romans 1:7a, ESV). *Be saintly because you are saints, as Paul says many times in his letter to the Romans.*

80

Just as you used to offer yourselves as slaves to impurity and to ever-increasing wickedness, so now offer yourselves as slaves to righteousness leading to holiness (Romans 6:19b). *Given that Christ has already sanctified us, a better translation might be "unto holiness" as in, "Just as you used to live unto wickedness when you were wicked, live unto holiness now that you are holy."*

But now that you have been set free from sin and have become slaves to God, the benefit you reap leads to holiness, and the result is eternal life (Romans 6:22). *A better translation may be, "have fruit unto sanctification." Holy fruit are reaped not manufactured. Like eternal life, fruit are gifts, not wages (John 3:16, 5:21).*

To the church of God in Corinth, to those sanctified in Christ Jesus and called to be His holy people ... (1 Corinthians 1:2a). *You are sanctified so act like it.*

Put to death, therefore, whatever belongs to your earthly nature: sexual immorality, impurity ... (Colossians 3:5a). *If you're a butterfly, don't act like a caterpillar. If you have been given a new nature, don't act in accordance with your old nature. That's hypocrisy. It's pretending to be someone you are not.*

It is God's will that you should be sanctified: that you should avoid sexual immorality ... (1 Thessalonians 4:3). *It is God's will that you should be sanctified in your conduct, not because your salvation hinges on it, but your wellbeing does. Sin is destructive.*

Each of you should learn to control your own body in a way that is holy and honorable, not in passionate lust like the pagans, who do not know God (1 Thessalonians 4:4–5). *You know who your Father is so don't act like someone who doesn't.*

May God Himself, the God of peace, sanctify you through and through (1 Thessalonians 5:23a). *Sanctification is God's work, not yours. Just as His gift of salvation is something to work out in your life, so is His sanctification. You already have it, so enjoy it!*

81

But just as He who called you is holy, so be holy in all you do (1 Peter 1:15). *You are not holy because you act holy. You are holy because you are children of a holy Father. Indeed, you are a holy nation (1 Peter 2:9). Be who you truly are.*

Chapter 8: Find out what pleases the Lord

Is God always pleased when He looks at us? Is He ever disappointed with us? These are the sorts of questions that divide those who preach radical grace from those who oppose it.

> Hyper-grace preacher: "We are totally pleasing in our Father's sight."
> Dr. Brown: "It is absolutely false to claim that when God looks at us, He always 'loves what He sees.'" (page 112)

The difference is the hyper-grace preacher is talking about *you*, while Dr. Brown is talking about *the things that you do*.

"Paul, isn't this just splitting hairs?" No. It's the difference between life and death! It's the reason why so many believers are messed up, worn out, and confused.

The issue here is identity. The relevant question is, *Who am I?* Your answer to this question will shape your life. For instance, if you define yourself by what you do, then your identity will only be as secure as your behavior. You'll think, "If I do good, God will smile at me, but if I don't, He won't."

This is an inferior way to live. You are not what you do and your value to God is not defined by your productivity or performance. You may be a pastor or a professor or a prostitute or a pill-popping prodigal but that is not who *you* really are. You are much more than that. You are a beloved child of the Most High God. This is the stunning revelation of the gospel.

> And suddenly a voice came from heaven, saying, "This is My beloved Son, in whom I am well pleased."
> (Matthew 3:17, NKJV)

82

Before Jesus had done a blessed thing—before He had preached the gospel or healed the sick or raised the dead—He received the loving affirmation and pleasure of His Father. How God relates to Jesus is how He relates to *you*. He loves you without any regard for your behavior. Your good deeds don't make Him love you more, and your bad deeds don't make Him love you less.

This issue of identity is so important, that I wrote a whole book about it. I wrote *The Gospel in Ten Words* so that you might know that your Father loves you 100 percent and is thoroughly pleased with you. He never changes His mind. Just as your behavior does not alter the sunlight falling on the earth, your behavior cannot alter the white-hot love of your Father for you. This is the gospel that Jesus preached:

> As the Father has loved me, so have I loved you. Now remain in my love. (John 15:9)

The danger is not that God will change His unchangeable mind and start hating you. The danger is that you won't remain in His love. If you're constantly hearing that God's approval of you goes up and down like the stock market you may begin to doubt His goodness. You may think, "I did good today, He loves me," or "I did bad today, He loves me not." You'll become an insecure and unstable believer.

It is critically important that you draw a big fat line between *who you are* (your Father's dearly loved child) and *what you do*. Dr. Brown appears not to make this distinction for he says "our heavenly Father ... does *not* always take enormous pleasure in us" (page 120). This is not true. He may not take enormous pleasure in some of your choices, but *you* He loves.

You only need to look at your own children to know this is true. I look at my kids with 100 percent, undiluted pleasure. My kids are the greatest kids on earth. I almost feel embarrassed that God gave me such great kids because the rest of you are missing out. Does this mean I am 100 percent happy with the choices my children make? Not at all. Was I pleased yesterday when my young son disobeyed his mother's command and ran onto the road? No, I was very displeased with his behavior. But with *him* I am and always will be well-pleased. How is this not obvious to every father?

As much as we love and appreciate our own kids, God loves us even more—much, *much* more. He's not coming second in any Father of the Year competition.

Pages 115–6: I love these two pages. Dr. Brown is preaching pure, sweet grace here! If you were to cut out these two pages and combine them with Dr. Brown's story about his forgiving father (page 3), and his testimony of living with a 24/7 assurance of God's love (page 12), you'd have a ready-made hyper-grace book. Now *that* would be a great book!

This is what I mean when I say every Christian has encountered the hyper-grace gospel. Dr. Brown surely has for he loves Jesus and raves about grace, particularly in chapter 1. The problem is not that we are preaching a different Jesus; the problem is that some are adding things to the gospel of Jesus. Instead of proclaiming "Christ alone," some are saying, "Christ plus confession, rule-keeping, and the pursuit of holiness." They don't understand that anything we add to Christ's perfect sacrifice diminishes it. Grace plus works don't mix.

The hyper-grace gospel is no new revelation. It is an old revelation buried under manmade traditions, religious rituals, and unholy packaging. Hyper-grace preachers aren't preaching a new and "modern" grace message, but an old and timeless one.

In this book I quote from more than 40 hyper-grace preachers all preaching essentially the same gospel. It's the same message from different messengers. This is a sign to make you wonder. How is it possible that Evangelicals and Charismatics, Catholic priests and Anglican vicars, rock stars and soldiers, theologians and poets, are all preaching the same gospel? The reason is we have all dug down to the same Treasure. Our rubble may be different, and some of us have bigger piles than others, but we have found a common Treasure.

How is it that pilgrims, all starting from different origins and traveling different paths, have ended up at the same place? The reason is we have all followed the same star that has led us to Jesus. Our baggage may be different, and some of us have more than others, but we have all arrived at the same Destination.

It doesn't matter where you start. What matters is where you finish. If you're digging through religious rubble, keep digging. And if you're walking through a wilderness of works, keep walking. Don't stop until you find that Treasure and arrive at that Destination called Jesus. He is your final port of call. He is your resting place.

Page 119: Dr Brown says hyper-grace teachers have all but eliminated the Father's loving discipline. This is a strange claim to make since Joseph Prince talks about discipline and chastisement in chapter 6 of *Destined to Reign*, Andrew Wommack writes about it in chapter 9 of *God Wants You Well*, and Bob George writes about it in chapter 13 of *Classic Christianity*. And these are just the books I found within the space of a few minutes. Personally, I have written several articles on the subject of Biblical correction, and a chapter entitled "How does God deal with us when we sin" can be found in my book *The Gospel in Twenty Questions*. Possibly what Dr. Brown means to say is that hyper-grace teachers don't teach discipline the way *he* would teach discipline, which is probably true.

On the bottom of page 119 Dr. Brown quotes a scripture that seems to be proclaiming conditional acceptance:

> Therefore "Come out from them and be separate, says the Lord. Touch no unclean thing, and I will receive you." And "I will be a Father to you, and you will be my sons and daughters, says the Lord Almighty." (2 Corinthians 6:17–18)

According to Dr. Brown, God is saying you need to "be very careful with how you live." But what if you're *not* careful? What if you make a mistake and stumble? What will happen then? Dr. Brown doesn't say but the outcome seems clear. Touch some unclean thing (whatever that is) and God will no longer be your Father.

This is a horrific thing to tell a child and it's not what Paul is saying here. If it were, he would be contradicting what he writes elsewhere when he says "Christ accepted you" (Rom. 15:7).[22]

Paul is not saying we purify ourselves to *become* His children. Instead, we purify ourselves because we *are* His children. He is saying the same thing as John says here:

Dear friends, now we are children of God, and what we will be has not yet been made known. But we know that when Christ appears, we shall be like Him, for we shall see Him as He is. All who have this hope in Him purify themselves, just as He is pure. (1 John 3:2–3)

Some people read the scriptures on purification and conclude, "I have to separate myself and withdraw from the world." But that's how cults form. That is not what Paul is saying at all. He's saying, "Don't get caught up in worldly concerns. Don't let this world pull you down from your lofty seat."

Jesus never told His disciples to withdraw from the world. In fact, He sent them *into* the world while praying that God would "sanctify them in it" (see John 17:15–18).

Page 121: Dr. Brown refers to the sinning Corinthians to show how God is sometimes displeased with us. "Your meetings do more harm than good." But *you* are not *your meeting*. Your value is not determined by how well you meet or preach or parent or drive your car. Even when chiding them over their poor communion habits Paul never disparages the Corinthians. He never calls them sinners or unforgiven Christians. Instead, he calls them "my brothers and sisters" reminding them that their value to him and God is unaffected by their behavior (1 Cor. 11:33).

Page 122: Dr. Brown writes that the "Corinthians were getting sick or even dying because they partook of the Lord's Supper in an unworthy manner." Along with other hyper-grace preachers, I totally reject the implication that doing communion wrong can kill you. That is not what Paul was saying in 1 Corinthians 11.[23]

Page 123: In 1 Corinthians 11:28, Paul says, "A man ought to examine himself." The mixed-grace preacher says, "You'd better check yourself for sin and make sure you're worthy enough to partake of communion because if you don't you could get sick and die." This is a graceless interpretation. The word for examine in this passage means "to test and by implication approve."[24] Paul is not saying, "Better make sure you're a real Christian." It doesn't work like that. In the old covenant, the high priest examined the sacrificial lamb, not the one who brought it. In the new covenant,

Christ is your Lamb without blemish or defect (1 Pet. 1:19). Paul is saying examine *Him.* See yourself as tested and approved in *Him.*

Page 123: Dr. Brown writes, "According to the modern grace preachers, Jesus says, 'I see each of you as beautiful, holy, and righteous, and I love what I see.'" Then I guess according to mixed-grace preachers, Jesus says, "I see each of you as ugly, unholy, and unrighteous, and I hate what I see." Which of these two messages sounds like good news to you?

To be fair, Dr. Brown says no such thing. I make this contrast merely to highlight the ambiguity of any mixed-grace message. Such a message will always leave you uncertain about your standing before God, while the hyper-grace gospel will leave you in no doubt that when Jesus looks at you, He loves what He sees. He may not love what you are doing, but *you* He loves and always will.

Dr. Brown asks, Why did Jesus confront issues in five out of the seven congregations in Asia Minor? Probably because He loved them. Isn't that His reason for doing everything?[25]

Page 126: Dr. Brown quotes Ephesians 5:1; "Be imitators of God, therefore, as dearly loved children." What a wonderful affirmation of your identity! When you know how much your heavenly Father loves you and is pleased with you, you won't be scared by warnings about being "very careful with how you live." May your Father's perfect love cast out all fears and insecurities!

Why does the Bible exhort us to find out what pleases the Lord? Because doing so will lead you straight to Jesus who is the embodiment of the Father's love to you. What pleases the Lord? It pleases the Lord to love you and to have you walk in His love every day of your life.

Chapter 9: Is spirituality effortless?

When Joseph Prince released his book *Destined to Reign: The Secret to Effortless Living* back in 2007, there was a backlash against his use of the word "effortless" in the subtitle. "The Christian life is not effortless," said some. "It's sheer, hard work."

Dr. Brown would agree for he quotes a preacher who says ministers must pray in "bloody sweat" and their intercession must touch "the point of agony"(page 128). Later in the chapter, Dr. Brown quotes J. C. Ryle who described the Christian life as one characterized by warfare and wrestling and who said "we must fight till we die" (page 147). According to Dr. Brown, the Christian life is anything but effortless. "This Christian walk requires effort!" (page 140). So Joseph Prince and other hyper-grace preachers who speak of effortless Christianity must be wrong.

What would Joseph Prince say in response to this?

> There are some religious people who get very uncomfortable when I use the word "effortless." "What do you mean there is no effort?" they argue. My reply is simple—a healthy tree bears good fruit without any strain, effort, or stress. When you are planted in the fertile soil of God's Word and His grace, fruits of righteousness will manifest effortlessly out of your relationship with Him. It's an inevitability! You cannot touch His grace and not become holy any more than you can touch water and not get wet.[26]

The strange thing is Dr. Brown partly agrees with this, for he says we are made righteous by grace (that's effortless) and he half-accepts that we are made holy by grace (also effortless). But then he also says our sanctification is something we have to work on (not effortless) and he quotes men who say "as soon as we cease to bleed we cease to bless" (definitely not effortless). It seems that Dr. Brown is promoting a mixture of effortless and effort-based Christianity.

Pages 129–30: Dr. Brown interprets Jesus' parable of the persistent friend as encouraging importunity in prayer (see Luke 11:5–8). "Jesus tells us to knock. A modern grace preacher tells us we need not knock. Who do we follow?" It depends. If you're outside, then knock. If you're inside, you don't need to knock.

John Sheasby says believers ought not to identify with the friend who is outside knocking, but with the children who are in bed with their father.

> The picture is of the warmth, closeness, and intimacy that is ours within the father's house. If the man reluctantly answers

the request of his friend on the outside, how much more eagerly will he answer the request of his children on the inside? ... We are not the friend on the outside; we are the children on the inside. Lying next to him. Snuggled warmly by his side. He is that near to us. And we are that dear to him.[27]

According to Dr. Brown, Sheasby has missed the point. We are not inside with the father, we are outside knocking. Yet I rather think it is Dr. Brown who misses the point for Jesus also tells us to ask and seek. He gives us a three-fold invitation. If you are lost, then seek. If you are outside, then knock.

The point of the parable is that God treats us better than we treat our friends. If we knock, says Jesus, the door will be opened, so stop knocking and come in. However, some interpret knocking as pounding on the gates of heaven with repetitive prayers. They think that if they pray and pray and pray, God will eventually give them what they ask for. But Jesus told us not to pray like that:

And when you pray, do not keep on babbling like pagans, for they think they will be heard because of their many words. Do not be like them, for your Father knows what you need before you ask Him. (Matthew 6:7–8)

Babbling on with repetitive prayers implies wearisome effort. "Don't pray to your Father like that," says Jesus. "Your effort doesn't impress Him. Instead, pray with the confidence that your heavenly Father loves you and delights to give good gifts to His children."

Page 131: Dr. Brown quotes Joseph Prince: "When you are under grace you will effortlessly fulfill and even super-exceed the expectations of the law of Moses." Dr. Brown wonders, "Is this true?" Well you'd better hope it's true because there's no way you're going to fulfill or super-exceed the righteous requirements of the law on the back of your own effort (see Rom. 3:20).

Dr. Brown wonders: "Is there such a thing as 'effortless spirit-uality'? If so, I would love to have more of it!" This is a startling request coming from one trying to refute those who would otherwise give him what he desires.

What does it mean to return to your first love? Dr. Brown interprets Jesus' words to the loveless Ephesians (in Rev. 2:1–7) as a recruiting campaign for effort-based Christianity. According to him, Christ's words "call for an intentional, effort-filled response."However, in a related note (see endnote 10 on page 267), Dr. Brown observes that at least one hyper-grace teacher claims that in the days of our first love we basically did nothing. Dr. Brown may be referring to something I wrote in *The Gospel in Ten Words*:

> The Ephesians were famous for their deeds yet Jesus basically said to them, "Stop what you're doing. Remember the height from which you have fallen and do the things you did at first."
>
> What were the things they did at first? Probably not much. I led a church for ten years and at the beginning we did little. We had no programs to keep us busy, no teams to manage, no leaders to train, no battles to fight, no website to maintain, and no vision to implement.
>
> What did we do with all our free time? We lived loved; we loved God, we loved each other, and we looked for ways to love our neighbors.
>
> True, my understanding of God's grace was a little mixed up, but we knew how to sit at the feet of Jesus and receive His love. Later, as the church began to grow, we got busy, sometimes to the point of distraction. But in the beginning we were more Mary than Martha.[28]

At the end of the day we will either follow Mary, who rested at Jesus' feet, or Martha, who tried to serve Him. Jesus tells us that Mary made the better choice.

Page 132: Those who preach effort-based spirituality like to quote Philippians 2:12: "Work out your salvation with fear and trembling." They would have you believe that your salvation is based on your works and since you can never be sure if you've done enough to merit salvation you should tremble and be afraid.

This works-based message is the antithesis of the hyper-grace gospel. To "work out" your salvation means to receive and rely upon the gift of grace that God has given you. Instead of living in reaction to the problems and trials of life, live in reaction to Jesus and what He has done. Make it your aim to see Christ revealed in your circumstances. Fear and trembling may be involved because faith often runs contrary to what our natural senses are telling us.

Pages 132–3: Dr. Brown wonders why hyper-grace preachers make such a sharp distinction between trusting in God's favor and relying on self-effort. We do it because the greatest temptation known to man is to mix grace with works and they just don't mix (Rom. 11:6).

Hyper-grace preachers such as Joseph Prince say, when it comes to trusting in self-effort or God's grace, there's no middle ground. It's one or the other. However, Dr. Brown says, "God's grace goes hand in hand with our obedience" (page 146). In other words, grace alone is not enough. You have to obey, contend, strive, wrestle, intercede, pray until you bleed, and fight until you die. How is this not mixing grace with works? How is this not repeating the mistake of the self-trusting Galatians? Dr. Brown may not be calling for circumcision, but he is certainly calling for effort. This is grace-killing foolishness.

> Are you so foolish? After beginning with the Spirit, are you now trying to attain your goal by human effort?
> (Galatians 3:3, NIV1984)

Grace-preachers will always encourage you to trust in God and His unmerited favor. Dr. Brown seems to have a problem with this. "Does that mean that we do nothing and just wait for God to do the work?" (page 133). Well if we didn't wait but ran ahead and did *something*, like Abraham did with Hagar, that wouldn't be trusting now would it?

The mixed-grace preacher says, "You have to do something," but the hyper-grace preacher says, "Jesus does it all." Spiritual fruit are not manufactured through toil and effort. Fruit grow naturally. There is nothing you can do to make His fruit appear but there is plenty you can do to hinder Him.

◢ Page 133: Apparently hyper-grace preachers only get it half-right; they don't preach "the whole counsel of God." (I wish I had a nickel for every time I've heard that line!) What is the whole counsel of God? Dr. Brown doesn't plainly tell us, but the apostle Paul does. In Acts 20 he says the whole counsel of God is the unmixed gospel of His grace. Period. Not grace plus your obedience nor grace plus self-effort. Just grace.[29]

Page 134: Dr. Brown repeats a complaint that is sometimes made against the modern grace message, which is that it makes people spiritually lazy. Although it's true that some people have misinterpreted grace as a license to be lazy, it cannot be fairly said that the grace message made them lazy. It is more accurate to say the grace message leads people to give up striving in their own strength and rest in Christ's finished work. Does this mean they become unfruitful and unproductive? On the contrary. As we saw in Part B, the fruit of love is not laziness but confidence and creativity (see Myth #12). When you know how much your Father loves you, you will be inspired to dream big dreams and attempt great things.

Pages 138–45: Dr. Brown lists several dozen scriptures that he feels call for self-effort. He over-reaches here for none of these scriptures actually says effort is required to make you spiritual, righteous, holy, or fruitful. Since he makes no attempt to explain how these scriptures are linked with spiritual outcomes, I'll only offer my thoughts on a few of them.

> And if your hand causes you to sin, cut it off. It is better for you to enter life crippled than with two hands to go to hell, to the unquenchable fire. (Mark 9:43, ESV)

What intrigues me about this verse is how those who use it to promote effort-based spirituality all have two hands! They don't actually practice what they preach. They excuse themselves by saying, "Jesus didn't really mean what He said. Allow me to reinterpret His words to a level just below what I have accomplished on my own." How is this not hypocrisy? The grace-preacher, in contrast, takes Jesus at His word. Jesus said what He meant and meant what He said every time.[30]

> We must go through many hardships to enter the kingdom of God. (Acts 14:22b)

Paul is not saying we have to jump through hardship hoops to qualify for the kingdom — that's the pagan doctrine of asceticism that Paul expressly rejected (see Col. 2:20–23). Rather, he's paraphrasing what Jesus said about having troubles in this world (in John 16:33). Paul is saying, "We Christians go through trials and tribulations from time to time." And he should know. Just three verses earlier Paul had been stoned and left for dead for preaching the hyper-grace gospel!

> Flee from sexual immorality ... (1 Corinthians 6:18a)

We don't flee from sexual immorality to become righteous or holy. We flee because sexual immorality is a bad idea. It will hurt you and those you love.

> Dear friends, I urge you, as foreigners and exiles, to abstain from sinful desires, which wage war against your soul.
> (1 Peter 2:11)

We don't abstain from sinful desires to become righteous or holy. We abstain because such desires war against our souls. Give into them and they'll mess you up.

> I came to cast fire on the earth, and would that it were already kindled! I have a baptism to be baptized with, and how great is my distress until it is accomplished! (Luke 12:49–50, ESV)

Jesus is distressed because He's about to be tortured and crucified. If you were about to be tortured and crucified you'd be distressed too. To suggest on the back of this verse that you have to go through crucifixion-like suffering to accomplish spiritual goals is thoroughly heathen.

Effort-based spirituality is an insult to Jesus and His matchless sacrifice. Jesus bled so that you don't have to. He died so that you might live and have life in abundance.

Chapter 10: Is God always in a good mood?

Grace preachers like to say, "God is always in a good mood." But Dr. Brown wonders, "Is He really? Was God in a good mood when He drove Adam and Eve out of the Garden or when Cain murdered his brother?" (my paraphrase of pages 152–3).

Dr. Brown frets that "modern grace teachers want us to focus almost exclusively on God's kindness, as if there were no possibility that His severity could ever apply to us" (page 152). He worries that we don't wave the sticks that keep Christians in line. We don't warn believers about the possibility of being hacked off from the vine and thrown into the fire.

Like most mixed-grace preachers, Dr. Brown doesn't seem to appreciate that in Christ we are eternally unpunishable. Since God dealt severely with all our sin on the cross (Rom. 8:3), He will never deal severely with us. Indeed, He cannot, said Spurgeon, without acting unjustly:

> How shall the Lord punish twice for one offense? If Christ took my sins and stood as my substitute, then there is no wrath of God for me … [31]

You may ask, "But what about those Jewish branches that were broken off because of their unbelief?" I know some people use Romans 11:20 to say you can lose your salvation, but Paul was referring to groups—Jews and Gentiles—rather than individuals. "I am talking to you Gentiles" (Rom. 11:13).

The nation of Israel was broken off, but certain individual Jews (like Paul himself) were grafted in through faith. Conversely, the Gentiles as a group have benefited from the kindness of God, although individual Gentiles may yet miss out through unbelief.

Paul writes that "some of the branches were broken off" (Rom. 11:17). That sounds like he's describing some sort of divine judgment. But the reality is that the Israelites cut themselves off. "God did not reject His people … they stumbled … they were broken off because of unbelief" (Rom. 11:2, 11, 20). And even though they were broken off the Jews are still loved "on account of the patriarchs" and will be immediately grafted in if they do not persist in unbelief (Rom. 11:23, 28).

So when Paul says, "Do not be arrogant, but tremble. For if God did not spare the natural branches, He will not spare you either" (Rom. 11:20b–21), he is not threatening the secure believer. He's speaking to the Gentiles *as a group*. He is saying, "Don't boast over the Jews. You Gentiles have a window of opportunity, like they did, but it won't stay open forever."

The heading on page 156 — "A God of mercy and of wrath" — suggests that we need a more balanced picture of God. We need the goodness of the modern grace message as well as the wrath of hellfire religion. In other words, we need a *mixed* gospel because the hyper-grace gospel is unbalanced.

It is certainly true that grace preachers emphasize God's goodness above His wrathfulness. Then so did David when he wrote, "For His anger lasts only a moment, but His favor lasts a lifetime" (Ps. 30:5). The Lord was similarly unbalanced when, speaking through the prophet Isaiah, He contrasted His "little wrath" with His "everlasting kindness" (Is. 54:8, NKJV).

It is inaccurate and unbiblical to try balance God's love and wrath. The Bible throws its weight on one side of the scales when it says, "God is love" (1 John 4:16). Everything He does is an expression of His love for us, even His wrath. If the wrath of God scares you, then you have the wrong picture of wrath because there is no fear in love.

Page 159: Dr. Brown writes: "My question to my hyper-grace friends is this: If you believe God's wrath is coming, why do you hardly ever (if ever) speak about it?" Actually we do speak about it. I, for one, have written extensively on hell, wrath, and judgment. Dr. Brown knows this for he challenges my claim that the condemnation of hell has no place in the gospel. He writes, "Of course the condemnation of hell has a place in the gospel of grace. In fact, it underscores the gracious message of the cross, since we all deserved hell because of our sins" (page 165).

A word about words seems appropriate here. *Gospel* means good news. I know there are some who think hell may be a place of refining, but many of us would agree that hell, whatever it is, is bad news. Since by definition there can be no bad news in the good news, the condemnation of hell has no place in the great and glorious announcement of what Christ has done. Certainly, God has saved us from something hellish, but as I explained in Part B (see Myth #11), what He has saved us *to* is infinitely greater than what He has saved us *from*.

Chapter 11: Marcion revisited

Marcion was a heretic who rejected the Old Testament along with most of the Gospels. Marcion taught that the God of the Old Testament was different from the God of the New Testament. Apparently "the spirit of Marcion lives on" in those who preach the modern message of grace and "follow the error of his ways" (page 182). This is a preposterous accusation.

Who, exactly, is following Marcion? Which hyper-grace preacher is saying there are two gods? Dr. Brown doesn't say. Instead he vaguely refers to some "Christian leaders" who make a contrast between the God of the Old Testament and the God of New Testament even though they believe, unlike Marcion, there is only one God (page 167).

Since Dr. Brown provides no evidence of hyper-grace preachers who teach a muddled, Marcionite message, I see no need to respond to his baseless claim.

But while we're on the subject, what do hyper-grace preachers say about the God of the Old Testament? We believe the God of the Old Testament is the same God who sits on the throne of grace and who, out of the fullness of His grace, sent us His Son Jesus. But while *we* know that the God of the Old Testament is our heavenly Father, those living at that time did not know, and this is reflected in their writings.

Andrew Wommack writes:

> In the Old Testament, we see a picture of God that is incomplete. It is not incorrect; it is just incomplete.[32]

The Old Testament picture of God is incomplete because the Old Testament was written by people who related to God through a law-keeping covenant. They described God as the Creator, *El*

Shaddai, the Ancient of Days, and so forth, but none of them thought of God as their heavenly Father. Before Jesus came, nobody referred to God as Father. This is why Jesus said:

> No one has seen the Father except the One who is from God; only He has seen the Father. (John 6:46)

Until Jesus showed up, no one really knew what God was like. The only person who can accurately explain God is God Himself, and He did this by sending us His Son. Jesus is God explaining Himself to the human race.

I am sometimes asked, "How does the angry God of the Old Testament fit with the nice God of the New?" This question makes it sound like there is more than one God or that God has mellowed with age.

> But the truth is God never changes. God has always been our loving Father. The first man, Adam, was called a son of God (Luke 3:38). The problem is not that God stopped being our Father. The problem is we ran away from home. The so-called "God of the Old Testament" is a fuzzy photograph taken with a telephoto lens by those who could not appreciate what they were looking at. Moses, Elijah, and the other Old Testament prophets had a revelation of God but they did not fully know Him.[33]

Before Jesus came, nobody did (John 1:18).

Cornel Marais has written, "What we think about Him comes from what we know about Him, and what we know about Him determines how we relate to Him."[34]

This is why we have it better than the righteous men and women of the old covenant. They did not know who their Father was but we do. Because of Jesus, we get to relate to Him as dearly loved children.

Pages 168–70: Dr. Brown seems to be of the opinion that hyper-grace teachers have little regard for the Old Testament. As we saw in Part B, this is a common misperception that seems to confuse the Old Testament with the old covenant (see Myth #7).

Hyper-grace teachers agree with the author of Hebrews who described the old covenant as obsolete and outdated (Heb. 8:13). We also agree with Paul who said all Scripture is useful for instruction in righteousness (2 Tim. 3:16). There is no contradiction here for the old covenant points to Christ who is our righteousness from God.

Page 172: Dr. Brown observes that, in contrast with modern grace preachers, the apostles often quoted from the Old Testament. What else could they do? The New Testament hadn't been written yet.

Page 173: Dr. Brown's claim that we're not preaching the Old Testament is undermined by his observation that the New Testament is packed with Old Testament references. Preach the New and you *are* preaching the Old.

To be honest, I don't think Dr. Brown is worried that we are modern Marcionites. Nor is he seriously concerned about how much of the Old Testament we may be preaching. I suspect his real concern is that we are "ignoring many of the lessons and warnings of the Hebrew Scriptures" (page 179). To some degree this is true. We don't preach the warnings and curses of the old law-keeping system because "Christ redeemed us from the curse of the law by becoming a curse for us" (Gal. 3:13). Using the warnings of the Hebrew Scriptures as sticks to motivate proper behavior among those who have been justified by Christ is to insult the cross and set aside grace.

Page 180: Dr. Brown says if we deny and turn away from Jesus, He will deny and turn away from us. This is a classic threat of the mixed-grace message but it's not true. Jesus' warning about denying Him and being denied in return evidently didn't apply to Peter who denied the Lord *three times*. Nor does it apply to any Christian. Saint, you are one with the Lord and He cannot deny Himself.

People are fickle. We change our minds, we break our promises, and we regularly fail. Fourteen centuries of the law-keeping covenant proves this. But God is not like us which is why He made the new covenant with Himself. If the new covenant hinged on our faithfulness, it would not be new. It would be just like the old one.

Writing on 2 Timothy 2:12–13 Andrew Farley notes that:

> Our faithfulness to God is an *old*-covenant problem that is solved by the new. Under the new, God has accomplished the unthinkable: He has taken us out of the equation. Our salvation and our faithfulness are all about Him.[35]

Have you ever wondered why Peter was not lost on the night he denied the Lord? After all, that was a particularly bad day for Peter. His faith grew cold, he drifted away, and he even called down curses on himself. He was no longer standing firm, continuing in the faith, or seeking to please the Lord. He was doing none of the things that mixed-grace preachers say you must do. Yet Peter was not lost because the Son of God was interceding for him. Jesus prays for you too (1 John 2:1).

If you are worried about dropping the ball and losing your secure position in Christ, you need to get your eyes off yourself and fix them on Jesus. You need to believe the promises of God:

> Being confident of this, that He who began a good work in you will carry it on to completion until the day of Christ Jesus. (Philippians 1:6)

Page 181: By quoting some of the promises in the Old Testament, modern grace preachers are "virtually stealing them from Israel." Now I'm confused. Does Dr. Brown want us to mine the treasures of the Old Testament or leave them untouched for Israel? And does he not know that all the promises of God are ours in Christ Jesus?

> For no matter how many promises God has made, they are "Yes" in Christ. (2 Corinthians 1:20a)

Chapter 12: The law of the Lord is good

Who would disagree with the title of this chapter? Every grace preacher I know agrees with Paul who said "the law is holy, righteous, and good" (Rom. 7:12). Yet an oft-heard criticism made against hyper-grace preachers is that we are opposed to the law. As we saw in Part B, this is a complete falsehood (see Myth #6). One characteristic of hyper-grace preachers is that we esteem the law and the purpose for which it was given.

Dr. Brown writes that hyper-grace teachers "think of God's Law ... as bad or defective" (page 184). This is simply not true. Even the hyper-grace teachers that he quotes, such as Andrew Farley, say that the law is good. They even say it in the bits he quotes! "There's nothing imperfect about the law itself. It's without blemish."

On page 185, Dr. Brown alleges that Andrew Farley "denigrates the Law, along with the principles of moral living." He does? When did he do that? To denigrate is to criticize unfairly. I read these pages several times and could not find Farley saying anything remotely critical about the law. In fact, he says the opposite. He says that the law is good and without blemish.

The only thing I could see that Dr. Brown might take issue with was when Farley says "the law has no place in the life of a Christian." In other words, Dr. Brown disagrees with the *application* of the law.

Like many mixed-grace preachers, Dr. Brown seems to think Christians ought to live by the law and Biblical principles for living. This becomes clear when he refers to Paul's exhortations as "specific commands" that must be obeyed (page 186). For instance, in Colossians 3, "Paul gives a series of specific instructions (commands!), including: 'Wives, submit to your husbands.'" Oh boy. Do we really want to go there?

A hyper-grace teacher would say that Paul's exhortations are not commands like the Ten Commandments. Nor are they new covenant laws *you must obey* to be saved or sanctified. Why do we say this? Because Paul himself says it in numerous places (e.g., Rom. 6:14–15, 10:4, Gal. 5:18). If Paul says we are not under law, why would he give us law to be under? It makes no sense.

If there is no wisdom in insisting on rules for holy living, as Paul says in Colossians 2:23, why would he then insist on rules for holy living? He would be contradicting himself.

The instructions and exhortations of the new covenant are not to be read as commands *that must be obeyed*. So how are we to read them? Dr. Brown gives us a brilliant phrase when he calls them "house rules," on page 186. This is a most apt description.

Perhaps you have seen those "House Rules" posters that say things like, "In this house we love, laugh, listen, help others, say 'thank you,' and that sort of thing. That's what Paul is giving us in his letters. He's giving us the house rules for our Father's house of grace. He's painting a picture of the new and wonderful life that is ours to enjoy in Christ.

Just as you would not kick your children out of your home or deprive them of your fellowship if they neglected to laugh, listen, or say "thank you," nor will God punish you for failing to keep His house rules. That's not the way to read them. The only way you could interpret Paul's Rules as commands to be obeyed is if you approach them with a law-keeping mindset.

"But what about when Paul quotes one of the Ten Commandments in Ephesians 6? Doesn't that prove Paul was in the command-issuing business?" Not at all. Paul was in the grace-dispensing business which is why he selectively quotes from the old commandments.

Look at what Paul says:

> Children, obey your parents in the Lord, for this is right. "Honor your father and mother" — which is the first commandment with a promise — "so that it may go well with you and that you may enjoy long life on the earth."
> (Ephesians 6:1–3)

That is a wonderful promise lifted straight out of the law. But what about the flip-side? What if we don't honor our father and mother? What happens then?

> What the law says will happen: "Anyone who curses their father or mother is to be put to death" (Exodus 21:17).
> What Paul says will happen: "_____"

Do you see? Under the law you got carrots and sticks, but under grace, it's just carrots, and carrots which Jesus paid for.

While it is true that Jesus quoted the curse associated with this commandment in Matthew 15:4, He did so while talking to religious people and law-teachers living under the law. You are not under the law.

Jesus and Paul preached different parts of the same law to different audiences for different purposes. There's a wonderful symmetry here. One used the law to silence the self-righteous; the other used it to illustrate a timeless truth.[36]

Page 187: What does it mean to have the law written on our hearts? Does it mean memorizing the Ten Commandments as the Jews did? Does it mean God will miraculously write those ten laws on our hearts like giving us the answers to a test? If so, I think I'm going to fail the test. I've been a Christian for forty-plus years and I'm not sure I could list all ten laws accurately and in the proper order. Could you?

In his book *Grace Rules*, Steve McVey gives what I think is the best illustration of how God writes His laws on our hearts. Consider the laws governing the responsibilities of parents. These laws are good and righteous. They serve a noble purpose by helping to ensure children receive proper care and nutrition. Yet McVey confesses that he and his wife have never been to the courthouse to read these laws. There may be hundreds of laws governing parental responsibilities but they haven't read a single one. Yet he can confidently assert that they have fulfilled every one of those laws.

> In fact, we have gone above and beyond what the law requires. Do you know why? It's because we have related to our children on the basis of love![37]

This is something every parent knows. We don't keep the laws to please the authorities and we don't relate to our children on the basis of these laws. We relate to them on the basis of love and keeping the laws flows naturally from that love relationship. So why do we have these laws? Because not everyone loves their kids. The laws are for those who neglect or abuse their children. They are not for loving parents.

We also know that the law is made not for the righteous but for lawbreakers and rebels ... (1 Timothy 1:9a)

The laws in the Bible were not written for those who love Jesus. Contrary to what the legalist may tell you, keeping the laws to earn what He freely offers is a sign that you don't know the love of God. A legalist reads the laws of the Bible and sees threats and warnings. *Keep the laws or else!* But love makes no threats.

Pages 190–1: Hyper-grace preachers will tell you that you are free from the commandments and not obliged to observe Christian principles. Dr. Brown counters that choosing to be moral is not at odds with living in the Spirit. But in a manner of speaking, it is. If you are told you must "choose" to keep the commands to be holy or to avoid dire consequences, you are neither free nor under grace. Your choice is an illusion. You're just a religious donkey getting whacked with a stick.

You may ask, "If you hyper-grace preachers say we are free from the law, aren't you encouraging immorality?" Not at all. We're saying moral living is a fruit not a root. Walking in the Spirit (living by faith in Christ) always leads to moral living just as planting acorns leads to oak trees. However, the opposite is not true. Striving to be a good Christian by keeping the command-ments is trusting in self. It's a faithless way to live. Even though your intentions may be good, it's walking after the old way of the flesh.[38]

"But don't the laws and commandments of the Bible show us how to please the Lord?" No, they don't. Do you need a rule-book to show you how to love and please your spouse? Nor do you need a rule-book to love and please the Lord.

God does not want you to love Him because you have to or because it's written in the rules. He's not after your good behavior. He wants *you*.

If you don't settle this in your heart you may run from your husband Mr. Grace back to your former husband Mr. Law (Rom. 7:1–6). Live by the rules and you'll be cheating on Jesus (to quote Andrew Farley). You'll be walking in the footsteps of the law-abiding but faithless Pharisees.

Page 192: Dr. Brown writes: "Hyper-grace teachers create a false dichotomy between a grace-filled relationship with God and an obedient, commandment-keeping relationship with God." I wouldn't say we create a false dichotomy. I'd like to think we dig a Grand Canyon between two incompatible types of relationship:

Old covenant: commandment-keeping, law-based relationship
New covenant: grace-filled, love-based relationship

A mixed-grace preacher says, "If you're living under grace, prove it by keeping the law." But a hyper-grace preacher says, "Don't even try. It's grace or it's law but not both." Mix the new with the old and you'll end up with the benefits of neither.

Page 192: Dr. Brown quotes 1 Corinthians 7:19: "Circumcision is nothing and uncircumcision is nothing," to make the point that "Keeping God's commands is what counts." Is Paul saying we need to keep the old commands? And if so, what about the old command to be circumcised, which he says is nothing and doesn't count? It seems confusing. It seems to be a mixed message.

Circumcision is the key to making sense of this verse. Circumcision was the hot issue of Paul's day. Some said you had to do it; others said you didn't. Paul dismissed the argument as irrelevant. "Circumcision was only ever a shadow, not the reality. In Christ we have been circumcised and that circumcision was not done by the hands of men" (Col. 2:11, my paraphrase). If you insist on living by the commands, you're living in the shadow and not the reality.

"But what about when Paul says 'Keeping God's commands is what counts'?" Don't you see? In Christ we have kept and continue to keep the commands of God. Just as your circumcision was not done by the hands of man, neither is your command-keeping. It's totally a God-thing.

Yet some people won't believe it. They think the hyper-grace gospel is just too good to be true. "There must be something I can do to impress God," they say. "There must be *one* command I can keep." There is:

And this is His command: to believe in the name of His Son, Jesus Christ ... (1 John 3:23a)

You need to believe that Jesus fulfilled all the law on your behalf. You need to believe that because of Him, you are free from the sticks and curses of the law.

Pages 193–4: Dr. Brown takes issue with the claim made by some hyper-grace preachers, including myself, that Israel basically asked God to give them the law-keeping covenant. "Honestly, when I read statements like these, I wonder if we are reading the same Scriptures." Dr. Brown's incredulity is not baseless. The Bible does not actually say the Israelites twisted God's arm into giving them the law-keeping covenant. But neither does it say, as Dr. Brown does, that "God gave Israel His laws ... because He had given His promise to Abraham, Isaac, and Jacob, and it was all based on His grace and not their merit." Both conclusions are inferred.

Dr. Brown says God gave Israel His laws based on His grace. Since law and grace are mutually exclusive, this is confusing. There is no such thing as a grace-based law. It's one or the other. It's grace or it's law. It's more accurate to say that God gave us the law so that we might appreciate our need for grace.

The covenant God made with the Patriarchs was grace-based. God's blessings to Abraham's family were based on His promises, not theirs. This can be clearly seen in the exodus of Israel. On their flight from Egypt the Israelites complained and murmured but God did not treat them as their sins deserved. Instead He gave them grace.

The Israelites complained on the shores of the Red Sea and God blessed them (Ex. 14). They murmured at Marah and God blessed them again (Ex. 15). They grumbled in the desert and God blessed them *again* (Ex. 16). God did not bless Israel because they were faithful (they weren't), but because *He* is faithful.

However, at Sinai, everything changed. The Israelites signed up for a law-based covenant where God's blessings now hinged on *their* faithfulness. They swapped the free bounty of heaven for the carrots and sticks of the law. It was the worst trade in history.

On the day they received the law the Israelites sinned again, but this time they paid a price and 3000 people died.

This is why I say Sinai was a bad day for the Israelites. Refusing to believe in the goodness of God — despite all the evidence of His grace — they asked for the stick and they got it.

The Israelites said, "We will do whatever you command us." Dr. Brown is impressed by their desire to obey the Lord. "It was a *good* response — the right response" (page 195). But it wasn't. It was a presumptuous and arrogant response.

The Israelites already had a covenant with the Lord, a grace-based covenant. But instead of trusting in God's faithfulness, which they had witnessed again and again, they opted to trust in their own. "We will do whatever you command us" was not a good response but a catastrophically bad one. As Joseph Prince has said, the Israelites fell from grace at Mt Sinai. "Man presumed on his ability" and the result was idolatry and death.[39]

Page 197: Dr. Brown writes: "I can't tell you how deeply it grieves my spirit when I see the Bible being radically reinterpreted to support a particular doctrine ..." This sentiment is shared by grace-preachers. To see the life-giving words of Jesus being turned into death-dealing commands or the old covenant law being used to beat God's kids is heart-breaking.

Page 200: Dr. Brown takes issue with grace preachers who don't follow the example of the Puritans by preaching the law to sinners. Well neither did Jesus. Although Jesus preached the law to the religious, there is no evidence He ever preached law to the tax-collectors, adulterers, or sinners that He regularly ate with. Usually He gave them radical, hyper-grace and it was His grace that changed them.

Page 201: Dr. Brown overreaches when he says the words love and grace are not found in any sermon preached in the book of Acts. The implication is that we should drop all mention of love and grace from our sermons and preach more on "self-control and the coming judgment," as Paul did to the corrupt governor Felix. To this I have three responses.

First, Dr. Brown's claim is a little misleading for the grace of God drips from the pages of Acts (e.g., Acts 4:33, 11:23, 14:3, 15:11, etc.). Second, Dr. Brown's implicit recommendation is at odds with Paul's explicit goal of "testifying to the gospel of God's grace" (Acts 20:24). Paul spoke of God's grace everywhere he went. Whenever people responded to grace he typically urged them to continue in it and not fall for some mixed-up message of grace plus works (see Acts 13:43 and Galatians). Third, Paul's message of judgment to the corrupt governor Felix bore no fruit. All it did was fill Felix with fear (Acts 24:25). It's easy to make people afraid by preaching about hell and judgment and you may even scare some into making a decision for Christ. But fear is a poor basis for any relationship.

Page 202: Dr. Brown writes: "It is clear that we must recover a love and appreciation for God's Law, along with the New Testament commands for living, if we are to be in harmony with Him." How is this not a subtle form of legalism? Any time you sell the blessings of God, whether it's righteousness, holiness, or harmony with Him, for the price of a little command-keeping, you're promoting works-based Christianity. It's a flesh trip.

The gospel of reconciliation is not, "Keep the rules, steer clear of sin, and you'll be in harmony with God." The gospel is, "God has reconciled the world to Himself through Christ and is no longer counting your sins against you" (see 2 Cor. 5:19).

Chapter 13: Why are we running from the words of Jesus?

Who's running? In this chapter Dr. Brown claims that hyper-grace preachers reject the pre-cross teachings of Jesus. Apparently, we steer people away from the Sermon on the Mount, we say the most popular verse in the Bible (John 3:16) is not for us, and the parables of Jesus are law sermons. These are astonishing accusations but, as we saw in Part B, they are all based on a misperception (see Myth #8). The truth is, hyper-grace preachers love the words of Jesus. How could we not? Jesus is the Lord of grace. He is the good news that we preach.

Dr. Brown says hyper-grace teachers dismiss the teachings of Jesus as old covenant. Although there is a measure of truth behind this claim, you will not find Joseph Prince, Andrew Wommack, or any prominent hyper-grace teacher saying, "the words of Jesus are not for us today" (page 203). If they did, Dr. Brown would surely quote them in his book.

Page 204: A question which confuses some people is: When did the new covenant begin? A hyper-grace preacher will tell you the new covenant began at the cross, not in Matthew chapter 1. Andrew Farley has said this and Dr. Brown is shocked. "Really?" But Farley was repeating something Jesus said on the night before He died.

> Jesus: "This is my blood of the covenant, which is poured out for many for the forgiveness of sins" (Matthew 26:28).
> Farley: "The new covenant did not begin at Jesus' birth but at His death."[40]

Oddly, Dr. Brown agrees with Farley ten pages later when he says Jesus ratified the covenant with His blood when He died on the cross (page 214). So why does he play the role of the shocked lawyer at the start of his chapter? Farley's statement is unambiguous and wholly based on the words of Jesus. If anyone is being dismissive of Christ's words here, it is not the grace preacher.

Page 205: Dr. Brown indulges in a little sarcasm by saying that modern grace teachers would have you ignore some of the classic sayings of Jesus. It's mildly entertaining but it's ham-fisted and unhelpful. This discussion adds nothing to Dr. Brown's charges against us and only reinforces common misperceptions.

Page 207: Dr. Brown writes: "Modern grace teachers would have to say John 3:16 is not the gospel and is not 'new covenant.'" Since John 3:16 is one of the foundational scriptures of the hyper-grace gospel this is a baffling thing to say. It's like saying Mozart hated music or Shakespeare hated poetry. Dr. Brown seems to think that grace teachers have taken a hatchet to everything written in the Bible prior to the cross.

Page 208: Dr. Brown quotes Ryan Rufus who said, "Unless you really understand grace, don't go near the Beatitudes. They will mess you up!" Again, Dr. Brown is shocked. *How can a respected preacher diss the Beatitudes?* But who's dissing the Beatitudes? Not Ryan Rufus. Look at his words again: "Unless you really understand grace, don't go near the Beatitudes." Why is this bad advice? The Beatitudes are the words of Jesus and they point to Jesus. If you read these words and see something other than Jesus, you will have missed their significance.

Consider the fourth Beatitude:

> Blessed are those who hunger and thirst for righteousness, for they will be filled. (Matthew 5:6)

If you don't understand grace, you may interpret Jesus' words as a call to get hungry and thirsty. But if you do understand grace, you will realize that Jesus is giving us a promise about Himself. He is the Righteousness you and I both need. He is the meal that truly satisfies.

I have written about this Beatitude elsewhere:

> The word for "filled" means gorged, indicating that the Chef of Heaven serves hearty dishes. He is not stingy with grace. When you partake of His righteousness you are filled to the point of satisfaction. When you eat the Bread of Life you get a meal that sustains and nourishes you for eternity. You will never hunger again.[41]

Miss grace and you will miss the Beauty behind the Beatitudes. Jesus is not saying "hunger is a virtue" or "being in a constant state of thirst is a good thing." He is saying those who are honest and open about their needs and the needs of this world will be satisfied because God promises to meet all our needs in Christ Jesus. He's saying, only those who are hungry and thirsty can receive the blessings of His grace.

I like what Brian Zahnd says about the Beatitudes:

> The Beatitudes are not advice or instructions or qualifications. They are nothing like that. They're not dictates or laws; the Beatitudes are *announcements*.[42]

In the same way that the gospel is an announcement, the Beatitudes are announcements. They are declarations of the Kingdom come. They are snapshots of the abundant life that is ours in Christ.

Page 211: Dr. Brown quotes Jesus' words about coming to Him for rest—"Come to me, all you who are weary and burdened ..." (Matt. 11:28–30)—and wonders, "Is a hyper-grace teacher going to tell me that these are 'old covenant' words that applied only to Yeshua's Jewish hearers?" Well, since I am a hyper-grace teacher, permit me to answer that question. "No, Michael, of course not." These words of Jesus are for all of us. They are particularly for those who are weary and burdened and looking for effortless spirituality, as you claim to be doing.

Page 212: Dr. Brown writes, "Don't believe those who tell you that Jesus preached the Law and Paul preached the gospel. Not so!" This leads into his point that Jesus and Paul both preached the gospel, which is true. But why is it untrue to say that Jesus also preached the law? Bizarrely, Dr. Brown says as much two pages later: "Did Jesus minister as a Law-abiding Jew to His fellow Jews? Of course He did" (page 214).

So what's the problem? The problem is Dr. Brown has been attacking a misperception for so long that he's actually come full circle and ended up agreeing with us.

Like many critics of the modern grace message, Dr. Brown is confused about what he is opposing. He says Jesus preached the law; we say Jesus preached the law. He says Jesus also preached the gospel; we say Jesus also preached the gospel. He says the new covenant was ratified on the cross; we say the new covenant was ratified on the cross. The only point of difference in this chapter is the imaginary one, the misperception that hyper-grace preachers are running from the words of Jesus.

Page 213: Dr. Brown writes that Jesus and Paul preached the same gospel of the kingdom. "When Paul preached the gospel of grace he was proclaiming the kingdom, and when Jesus preached the kingdom, He was proclaiming the gospel of grace." I find it hard to disagree with this since it's almost word-for-word identical to something I wrote several years ago:

The *gospel of the kingdom* is the *gospel of Christ* which is the *gospel of God* which is the *gospel of grace*. They are different labels for the exact same gospel message.[43]

Page 213: Dr. Brown writes, "How can hyper-grace teachers tell us that Jesus' faithful earthly followers received law upon law and harsh teaching upon harsh teaching?" We don't. We believe Jesus preached the law *and* He revealed grace. He gave law to those who were confident of their own righteousness and He gave grace to the poor and needy.

Page 214: Dr. Brown wonders how anyone could suggest that the parable of the prodigal son was a law story rather than a grace story. I don't know anyone who is suggesting this. Nor does Dr. Brown, for he names no names.

Instead of dismissing the parable of the prodigal son as law, most hyper-grace preachers hold it up as a brilliant illustration of the Father's radical grace. This parable features in many of our books: Watchman Nee wrote about it in chapter 7 of *The Normal Christian Life*; Steve McVey wrote about it in chapter 9 of *Grace Walk*; Joseph Prince wrote about it in chapter 12 of *Destined to Reign*; Tullian Tchividjian wrote about it in chapter 2 of *One Way Love*; I wrote about it in chapter 7 of *The Gospel in Twenty Questions*; Malcolm Smith wrote about it in many places in *The Lost Secret of the New Covenant*; and John Sheasby wrote an entire book about it called *The Birthright*.

Page 217: Dr. Brown writes, "Why do so many in the hyper-grace camp want to reject the words of Jesus?" Again, this is tilting at windmills. Who is rejecting the words of Jesus? If there are "so many" of us saying we should reject the words of Jesus, how is it that Dr. Brown can't find one of us who actually says this?

Dr. Brown has read our books. He knows that every prominent hyper-grace teacher quotes the words of Jesus extensively. How could we not? The gospel we preach is a revelation of Jesus Himself. To say that grace preachers reject the words of the one called Grace is like saying legalists reject the law. It's bizarre.

Page 219: Dr. Brown finishes his chapter with Jesus' warning about being "ashamed of me and of my words" (Luke 9:26). Given his allegations that hyper-grace teachers reject the words of Jesus,

111

this is no doubt meant as a warning for us. The implication is that Jesus will be ashamed of us when He returns. If so, then I guess we are fortunate indeed that Dr. Brown is not ashamed to call us his brothers!

Chapter 14: The new Gnostics

Gnostics believe there is more than one god and that the God of the Old Testament was not the Father of Jesus. In chapter 14 of his book, Dr. Brown throws a can of Gnostic paint over those who preach the hyper-grace gospel. Although he covers himself by saying he does not consider hyper-grace teachers such as Joseph Prince, Clark Whitten, and Andrew Farley to be modern-day Gnostics, he nevertheless names many of us in his chapter entitled "The New Gnostics." So if we're not the New Gnostics, who are?

I found this chapter a little fuzzy and hard to follow. It was hard to zero in on Dr. Brown's grievances, so if you want to skip ahead, I'll understand.

One of the issues that is raised in this chapter has to do with our fellowship with the Lord and how sin affects it. This issue can be framed with a question: Does wrongdoing take us out of fellowship with the Lord? Hyper-grace teachers, such as Steve McVey, say no; Dr. Brown says yes (page 223). It seems like a strong difference but there is possibly some talking at cross-purposes here. Consider these definitions of fellowship:

> Hyper-grace teacher: fellowship (*koinonia*) describes our union with Christ; your sin cannot break it
>
> Mixed-grace teacher: fellowship describes the daily experience of relating to the Lord; your sin can hinder it

As Steve McVey says, when you sin your perception of fellowship changes and you may think yourself estranged from the Lord, but from God's side nothing changes. "Fellowship is not about your feelings. It's about how we're related to God because of the finished work of Jesus Christ."[44]

Just as our good deeds didn't join us to the Lord in the first place, our bad deeds can never separate us from Him. According to Romans 8:38–39, nothing can. This is why Paul mentions the unthinkable proposition of uniting the members of Christ (us) with the members of a prostitute (1 Cor. 6:15–18). If such a thing were not possible, why would Paul tell us not to attempt it?

For Dr. Brown, however, fellowship means something different. It's more like the fellowship we experience at church on Sunday. Both he and McVey use the story of the prodigal son to illustrate how fellowship can or cannot be broken. So who's right? To some degree they are both right because they are talking about different things. Dr. Brown observes that the son did not experience fellowship with the father for as long as he was away from home, while Dr. McVey observes that the father at no time stopped relating to his son as a father.

Perhaps the more important issue here is how fellowship is restored. When you stumble and drift away from the Lord, you don't care about theological terms like *koinonia* or connate union. You just want to know how to make things right.

The prodigal son tried to fix his relationship himself. He had the mindset of works-based religion. *I broke it, I'll fix it.* The good news is that the father wouldn't let him fix it. He had no intention of interviewing his son for a job. He was just thrilled to have him back.

This is how it is with you and your heavenly Father. When you make mistakes you may perceive yourself as being out of fellowship with the Lord and you may buy into the lie that says you have to do something to make things right. *I have to confess my sins to repair the damage I've done.* But God doesn't see it like that. You're His kid in good times and bad times. You never stop being His kid and He will never take you on as a hired hand.

Grace-based confession is healthy. But if you confess sins because you fear your relationship with the Lord will be damaged if you don't or that God may withdraw from you in a holy huff, you're acting in unbelief. You're saying, "I broke it, I can fix it," which is exactly what Adam said when he reached for the fig leaves. The fact is, you didn't break it (your union with the Lord) and if you had (which you can't) you couldn't fix it anyway.

Page 227: Dr. Brown writes, "These hyper-grace teachers are telling us that we can walk in darkness, potentially for protracted periods of time, without walking away from the Lord or experiencing any break in fellowship with Him." Actually, that's not what we're saying. We're saying that our union with the Lord is not based on our faithfulness but His. *This* is the revelation that leads to holy living and healthy confession.

Those who know how much their Father loves them don't want to walk away. In contrast, those who think their relationship is based on how well they perform often do.

Page 232–3: I get mentioned for saying, "We are not our sins." Dr. Brown wonders, "What should we take that to mean? ... Using Dr. Ellis' logic, believers throughout the New Testament could respond to Paul and other leaders by saying, 'Why are you rebuking us? We are not our sins!'" Again, Dr. Brown seems to think it is unhelpful to distinguish between our identity and our behavior. I strenuously disagree. It is absolutely essential to separate *what you do* from *who you are*. Every loving parent knows this. When my kids misbehave, I don't say "*You* are unacceptable." I say "Your behavior is unacceptable." We kick habits, not children. We break mindsets, not minors.

Defining people by their behavior is a big part of the reason why many in the church are neurotic and insecure. We have been told that our heavenly Father is *not* pleased with us, that when He looks at us He *doesn't* love what He sees, and that it's up to us to make things right. This is a most odious and unbiblical teaching. Can you imagine walking into your child's room at night and saying such awful things?

You need to see yourself as the apple of your Father's eye. If God has a desk in His heavenly office, your photo's on it. If God loved you while you were a sinner, He surely loves you now. His love for you never changes. Plumb its depths, ascend its heights, for you will never reach its limit!

Page 233: I am grateful that Dr. Brown recognizes that hypergrace preachers such as Joseph Prince, Ryan Rufus, Clark Whitten, Andrew Farley, and myself are totally opposed to sin. It's a pity, then, that he seeks to discredit our message elsewhere (on pages 18 and 238) by saying it leads to sinful living.

Page 235: Dr. Brown notes that some hyper-grace believers claim they no longer sin. I can understand why he finds such a claim hard to swallow. But since we're on the subject, I would love to know what he and other opponents of the modern grace message make of these words from John:

> No one who lives in Him keeps on sinning. No one who continues to sin has either seen Him or known Him.
> (1 John 3:6)

As I explain elsewhere, there are two ways to read this passage.

> Someone schooled in the sticks and carrots of the old covenant will interpret these words as a threat. "If you want to remain in Him and stay saved, you had better stop sinning" ... However, John's remarks about not sinning should not be read as a threat but a promise. He is describing the new reality of the life we have in Christ. Jesus didn't sin and He never will. If you let Him live His life through you, then without any conscious effort on your part you're going to start talking and walking just like sinless Jesus. It's inevitable. Live with someone long enough and you begin to resemble that person in manner and thought. I am not saying your behavior will attain a level of sinless perfection this side of eternity. I am saying that living in fellowship with the sinless Son produces desires in us that are informed by His righteous nature. You are Sonful not sinful.[45]

Page 236: Hyper-grace preachers love to quote 1 John 4:17b: "As He is, so are we in this world" (NKJV). We say, "Since Christ is my identity, whatever is true of Him is true of me." But Dr. Brown isn't falling for this for a second. He knows where this sort of thinking leads. "Why not say: 'Since God is perfect, I am perfect'? 'Since God is sinless, I am sinless'?" But what are we supposed to say? That 1 John 4:17 is wrong? Or that Jesus is imperfect and sinful?

Dr. Brown seems to miss the point which is this. In Christ we get to choose how we live. Formerly, while we were prisoners of sin, we had no freedom to choose. Since anything that is not of faith is sin (Rom. 14:23), everything we did was stained with sin.

But now that we have received the Spirit of liberty, we get to choose. We can walk after the old way of the flesh or the new way of the Spirit. If you are walking in step with the Spirit, will you sin? If your eyes are fixed on Jesus, will you sin? I think not.

Jesus died to set you free and free people get to choose. It's a choice of living in one of two realities. We can live in an earthly reality characterized by our shortcomings and failings or we can live in the higher reality of the kingdom where we are seated with Christ in heavenly places. An old covenant preacher will lead you to focus on yourself and your shortcomings, but a new covenant preacher will inspire you to fix your eyes on Jesus and His sublime perfections. We are not changed by looking at ourselves. We are changed by beholding Jesus.

Page 237–8: Dr. Brown writes about a young man who claims to have redeemed profanity and who says swear words can be used as blessings. According to Dr. Brown, some hyper-grace adherents go off the deep end on account of errors mixed into the modern grace message. "It is a logical progression." If I was feeling uncharitable I could just as easily argue that there is a logical link between a mixed-grace gospel and all the worst evils of Christendom; evils far more serious than young men spouting obscenities on YouTube.

In any group of believers you will find some people doing odd things. But was Paul's gospel invalidated because a Corinthian man heard it and started sleeping with his father's wife? Was Jesus' message proved wrong on account of Judas' betrayal?

Arguing for a logical progression between the gospel of grace and sin makes as much sense as saying medicine leads to death. It's not only silly it's dangerous for it deters people from seeking the only remedy that can free them from the power of sin (see Rom. 6:14).

Chapter 15: The finished work of the cross

Like the term "hyper-grace" the phrase "finished work" means different things to different people. To a grace-teacher, "finished work" means mission accomplished. Everything that needed to be done to make you holy, righteous, and pleasing to God was accomplished at the cross. As Derek Prince has said, Christ's work is "perfectly perfect and completely complete."[46] You cannot improve upon it. All you can do is receive the benefits of it through faith.

But to a Universalist, the phrase "finished work" means something different. According to Dr. Brown, it means "every person will be saved" (page 240). Is this what hyper-grace teachers claim? No. This is what *Universalists* claim.

A totally illegitimate line of reasoning is presented in this chapter. It runs like this: "Grace preachers such as Joseph Prince preach on the 'finished work' of the cross. Universalists preach the 'finished work' on the cross. See the connection?" But there is no connection. None at all. Linking the hyper-grace gospel with the message of universalism in this way is bad scholarship and wholly unjustified. It does nothing but stir up strife and perpetuate misperceptions such as Myth #3 in Part B.

In this chapter Joseph Prince and Andrew Wommack are mentioned alongside notable Universalists as though they were all preaching the same message. I do not wish to make any judgments about the doctrine of universalism here except to say that most grace preachers, including Prince and Wommack, do not preach it. If anything they preach *against* it. Dr. Brown acknowledges as much when he says: "It is true that the great majority of modern grace teachers have not embraced this error (of universalism) ..." (page 245). If it's true, why bring it up? Why link hyper-grace preachers with it? What possible purpose could it serve in a book attacking the modern grace message except to make those of us who preach it guilty by association?

Page 242: Andrew Wommack says Jesus hasn't saved, healed, or delivered anyone in 2,000 years. "This, of course, is absolutely untrue," says Dr. Brown. He then provides a list of verses that show God saving, healing, or forgiving after the cross. But every one of these verses proves Wommack's point, which is that God provided everything you and I will ever need through the sacrificial death of His Son.

Faith appropriates what God has already provided. Faith doesn't move God; He isn't the one who is stuck. Faith doesn't make God do anything. Grace and faith work together, and our part is to accept what God has already done.[47]

In Acts 9:34, which is one of the scriptures Dr. Brown cites, Peter's faith appropriated what Christ has provided and the paralytic walked. Peter would later write,

> (Jesus) bore our sins in His own body on the tree, that we, having died to sins, might live for righteousness — by whose stripes you were healed. (1 Peter 2:24, NKJV)

Peter says you *were healed*. A sick person might respond, "This, of course, is absolutely untrue." But in a manner of speaking Peter and Andrew Wommack are spot on. Everything that you will ever need — every blessing of healing, forgiveness, deliverance, etc. — was made available to us through the finished work of Christ.

> Praise be to the God and Father of our Lord Jesus Christ, who has blessed us in the heavenly realms with every spiritual blessing in Christ. (Ephesians 1:3)

The hyper-grace gospel declares that we *have been* blessed in Christ. Asking God to provide salvation, healing, or deliverance is like asking Jesus to come and die again. It's failing to recognize that God has already blessed us "with every spiritual blessing in Christ." I'm not saying it's wrong to ask God for things. I'm saying we don't need to ask Him because He has already given us everything we need through Christ Jesus.

One of the most under-rated scriptures in the Bible is surely this one:

> I thank my God, making mention of you always in my prayers, hearing of your love and faith which you have toward the Lord Jesus and toward all the saints, that the sharing of your faith may become effective by the acknowledgment of every good thing which is in you in Christ Jesus.
> (Philemon 1:4–6, NKJV)

How do we make our faith effective? We don't do it by pounding the doors of heaven and asking God to give what He has already given. Nor do we do it by examining our lives for unconfessed and unrepented sin. Faith only becomes effective when we acknowledge the good things that are already ours in Christ Jesus.

Appendix: Once saved, always saved?

In closing his book, Dr. Brown writes about the possibility of losing your salvation and what to do about it if you have. If you have walked away from the Lord, "you have forfeited your salvation, so turn back to Him now, knowing that He is quick to forgive ..." (page 251). This sounds like you can be saved, unsaved, and then re-saved. It makes me think that

> Jesus is sitting in heaven with a pen in one hand and a bottle of correction fluid in the other. Get saved, name goes in. Fail a test, name goes out. Recommit your life to God, name goes back in. With all the recommitments going on, you'd think Jesus was in danger of repetitive stress injury.[48]

This is an absurd picture and one that is at odds with the many promises of God regarding your eternal security. The notion that you can lose your salvation and get re-saved is also inconsistent with Dr. Brown's own theology.

In various places in his book he insists that the warnings of Hebrews 10:26–29 about sinning and trampling the Son of God underfoot apply to *believers* (see pages 46 and 105). Sin as a Christian and you're in danger of the raging fire that will consume the enemies of God. Hebrews makes it plain that those who've tasted the goodness of God and fallen away cannot repent (Heb. 6:5–6). Yet Dr. Brown says you can. If you have forfeited your salvation, "turn back to Him now."

If Dr. Brown is correct about Hebrews elsewhere, then he must be incorrect here. Walk away from God and you cannot repent. However, if he's right in saying you can repent and get re-saved, then he must be wrong in saying the warnings of Hebrews apply to believers. He can't have it both ways.[49]

119

I don't point out these inconsistencies to embarrass Dr. Brown but to highlight the muddled thinking that is part and parcel of mixed-grace message. One week you'll hear a scripture presented as a carrot, but the next week the same scripture becomes a stick. One preacher says it's a glorious promise, the next says it's a sober warning. First it sounds like good news, then it sounds like bad news. The mixed-grace gospel is so confusing you need a PhD to figure it out.

Of course, those who trust in the hyper-grace gospel don't worry about these sorts of theological flip-flops because we don't trade in the market for carrots and sticks. If a certain scripture sounds like a curse, we look to Jesus who has redeemed us from every curse (Gal. 3:13). If another scripture sounds like a blessing, we say, "Thank you, Jesus, for in you we have received every blessing" (Eph. 1:3). And when it comes to eternal security we don't worry about the possibility of forfeiting your salvation, because those whom Jesus saves, Jesus keeps (1 Cor. 1:8).

Summary of *Hyper-Grace*

In summary, *Hyper-Grace: Exposing the Dangers of the Modern Grace Message* is a tale of two gospels; the hyper-grace gospel and the mixed-grace gospel. Dr. Brown's purpose in his book is to reveal the errors of the former by contrasting it with claims of the latter. However, his exposé falls short three ways.

First, his attempt to discredit the hyper-grace gospel is compromised by numerous misperceptions and misunderstandings. Although Dr. Brown positions himself as someone who is familiar with the hyper-grace message, the evidence suggests otherwise. In his book he perpetuates all twelve myths identified in Part B. Consequently, he spends considerable time attacking things hyper-grace preachers have never said.

Second, Dr. Brown makes a number of baseless accusations against those who preach the hyper-grace gospel. He claims we denigrate the law and reject the words of Jesus, yet he provides no evidence to support these claims. Instead of adding weight to his case, groundless charges such as these reinforce the impression that Dr. Brown is attacking a distorted version of our message.

120

Third, in disagreeing with those of us who preach the hyper-grace gospel, Dr. Brown aspires to be "fair and gracious" (page xiii). However, his desire for engagement is undermined by rhetoric that is sometimes inflammatory. His attempts to link us with sinners and Universalists are clumsy and baffling, while his allegations that we follow the error of Marcion and are the new Gnostics are antagonistic and unjustified.

Where Dr. Brown does succeed, however, is in portraying the main beliefs of the mixed-grace message, which are these: your sins are not forgiven unless you repent (chapter 4) and confess (chapter 5); the Holy Spirit uses the law to find fault with you and convict you of your sin (chapter 6); sanctification is something you have to work on (chapter 7); your heavenly Father is not always pleased with you (chapter 8); the Christian walk requires hard work, suffering, and effort (chapter 9); and finally, you need to be mindful of God's wrath because you could yet end up as His enemy (chapter 10).

To encourage you to embrace his message, Dr. Brown dangles the carrots and waves the sticks of DIY religion. He puts price-tags on grace and exhorts you to live by the law. He sends mixed messages about the love of God and puts big question marks over your eternal security.

Although Dr. Brown's book does a poor job of portraying and refuting the hyper-grace gospel, it does an excellent job of proclaiming the mixed-message of grace plus works.

I'll leave it to you to decide which is the good news.

Final Word

Everything about the hyper-grace gospel is extreme because your heavenly Father is extreme. His love for you is greater than you can possibly conceive or imagine. If you think you have a handle on the grace of God, you don't. The Bible declares His love and grace surpass knowledge. However grand or over-the-top you imagine His grace to be, His grace is greater still.

The unfathomableness of God's goodness towards us reminds me of a conversation Clark Whitten once had with a cosmologist. The two men were talking about how the universe is growing rapidly.

"The universe is expanding at the rate of 186,000 miles per second in all directions," said the cosmologist. "It has been doing so from the moment God spoke it into existence."

Having said this, the cosmologist asked a profound question.

"Do you know *why* it is expanding?"

Pastor Whitten confessed he did not know.

"Because it's not big enough," came the reply. What the cosmologist said next is startling. It will fry your mind and change the way you think about God.

The universe is expanding at the speed of light in all directions because it isn't yet big enough to contain all the things God has prepared for those who love Him![1]

Wow! That's the kind of Father you have. He's excessive, extreme, and over-the-top in ways that only He can be. Everything He does is very good and very great.

And that's the hyper-grace gospel!

Escape to Reality

If you still have questions about the hyper-grace gospel, you can find answers at Paul Ellis' website. Visit escapetoreality.org and you will discover:

- 400+ grace-based articles covering 700+ scriptures
- reviews of 50 outstanding grace books
- resources for private study and small group discussion
- hundreds of stories of lives radically changed by grace

Notes

Introduction
1. Philip Yancey, *What's So Amazing About Grace?* OMF Literature: Manila, Philippines, 1997, p.71.
2. D. L. Moody, *The Way to God and How to Find It*, Fleming H. Revell: Chicago, IL, 1884/1912, p.16.
3. Malcolm Smith, *The Lost Secret of the New Covenant*, Harrison House: Tulsa, OK, 2002, p.51.

PART A: The Hyper-Grace Gospel
1. The apostle Paul dedicated his life to the testifying to the "gospel of God's grace" (Acts 20:24) which he sometimes called the "gospel of Christ" (Rom. 15:19, Gal. 1.7).
2. Paul Ellis, *The Gospel in Twenty Questions*, KingsPress: Birkenhead, New Zealand, 2013, p.38.
3. The word Paul uses in Romans 5:20 is *huperperisseuo*, which is made up of two Greek words: The Greek word *huper* means the same thing as the English prefix hyper, while the verb *perisseuo* is related to the adverb *perissos* which means "superabundant." G4053 (*perissos*), Strong's Exhaustive Concordance, website: concordances.org/greek/4053.htm (accessed March 10, 2014). "Hyper," Oxford Dictionaries, Oxford University Press, website: www.oxforddictionaries.com/definition/english/hyper- (accessed March 10, 2014).
4. Meir Ben Isaac Nehorai wrote this poem in 1050. According to Ben Glanzer, the poem was forgotten until 1917 when it was found scrawled on the walls of a mental institution in the room of a man who had just died. Rediscovered, it was incorporated into a hymn called "The Love of God," by Frederick M. Lehman. Source: Ben Glanzer, "The Story of 'The Love of God,'" *Ministry*, website: www.ministrymagazine.org/archive/1950/09/the-story-of-the-love-of-god (accessed 27 March 27, 2014).
5. Watchman Nee, *The Normal Christian Life*, Tyndale: Wheaton, IL, 1957/1977, p.172.
6. D. Martyn Lloyd-Jones, *Spiritual Depression: Its Causes and Cure*, Wm. B. Eerdmans: Grand Rapids, MI, 1965, p.132.
7. Brennan Manning, *The Ragamuffin Gospel*, Multnomah: Sisters, OR, 1990/2000, p.26.
8. Here are some supporting scriptures for the Table. What is it? Rom. 11:6, Heb. 12:2, Jude 1:24. Grace is: John 1:14–17, Eph. 1:3, 7. Faith is: Rom. 10:17, 1 Th. 2:13, Phm 1:6. To repent (*metanoeo*) is to change one's mind, so repentance (*metanoia*) is literally a change of mind: Mark 1:15, Acts 20:21, 26:20, Rom. 2:4. To confess (*homologeo*) means to agree with another: Rom.

10:9–10. Forgiveness is: Ps. 103:12, Is. 43:25, John 1:29, Acts 13:38, Heb. 9:26, 1 John 2:2. Obedience is: John 14:15, 23, 15:9–11; 1 John 2:5. Sanctification is: 1 Cor. 1:2, 30, 3:16–17, 6:11. Be holy because: 1 Pet. 1:15, 2:9, 1 John 4:17. The law: Rom. 10:4, Gal. 3:24, 5:4, Php. 3:9. Sacrifice is: Heb. 10:5, 10–14. God's love is: Jer. 31:3, John 3:16, Rom. 5:8, 1 Cor. 13:4–8, Eph. 3:17–19. To convict (*elegcho*) literally means to expose (see Eph. 5:13). The Holy Spirit does this by bringing things into the light of God's truth: Ps. 103:10, John 16:13, Heb. 10:15–17. Eternal security hinges on: Is. 49:15–16, John 6:37, 14:16, Rom. 8:38–39, 1 Cor. 1:8–9, 2 Cor. 1:21–22. I am first and foremost: Rom. 8:15, Gal. 3:26, 4:6, 1 John 3:1. How to overcome sin: Rom. 6:6–7, 10–14, Gal. 2:20, Col. 2:11, 3:3. More gets done when I: John 15:4–5. This message makes me: Col. 3:1–2, Heb. 12:2.

9. Quoted in Michka Assayas, *Bono on Bono: Conversation with Michka Assayas*, Hodder: London, UK, 2005, pp.203–4.

10. What Watchman Nee actually said was: "We have spoken of trying and trusting, and the difference between the two. Believe me, it is the difference between heaven and hell." Source: Nee, *The Normal Christian Life*, p.183.

11. Quoted in R. C. H. Lenski, *The Interpretation of St. Paul's Epistle to the Romans 8–16*, Augsburg Fortress, Minneapolis, MN, 2008, p.746.

12. Attributed to Martin Luther by C. H. Spurgeon, *The Treasury of David: Psalm 126*, date unknown, website: www.spurgeon.org/treasury/ps126.htm (accessed February 20, 2014).

13. C. H. Spurgeon, "Redemption through blood, the gracious forgiveness of sins," Sermon No.2207, The Spurgeon Archive, 1891, website: www.spurgeon.org/sermons/2207.htm, (accessed March 10, 2014). Some people get upset when I quote Spurgeon in a hyper-grace context. But he was the one who said, "A sermon without Christ as its beginning, middle, and end is a mistake in conception and a crime in execution," which is exactly the sort of thing a hyper-grace preacher would say. Source: C. H. Spurgeon (1881), "Without Christ—nothing," Sermon No.1625, Spurgeon Gems, 1881, website: www.spurgeongems.org/vols25-27/chs1625.pdf, accessed March 14, 2014.

14. Smith, *The Lost Secret of the New Covenant*, p.57.

15. Andrew Wommack, *Grace: The Power of the Gospel*, Harrison House: Tulsa, OK, 2007, p.61.

16. Joseph Prince, *The Power of Right Believing: 7 Keys to Freedom from Fear, Guilt, and Addiction*, Faith Words: New York, NY, 2013, p.226.

17. Robert Farrar Capon, *The Mystery of Christ*, Wm. B. Eerdmans: Grand Rapids, MI, 1993, p.21.

18. Dudley Hall, *Grace Works*, Vine Books: Ann Arbor, MI, 1992, p.11.

19. Max Lucado, *Grace: More Than We Deserve, Better Than We Imagine*, Thomas Nelson: Nashville, TN, 2012, p.10.

20. Jerry Bridges, *Transforming Grace*, NavPress: n.p., 2008, p.21.

21. Tullian Tchividjian, *One Way Love: Inexhaustible Grace for an Exhausted World*, David C. Cook: Eastbourne, UK, 2013, p.36.
22. Benjamin Dunn, *The Happy Gospel: Effortless Union with a Happy God*, Destiny Image: Shippensburg, PA, 2011, p.88.
23. Judah Smith, *Jesus Is ___*. Thomas Nelson: Nashville, TN, 2013, p.126.
24. Paul White, *Revelation to Transformation*, Westbow Press: Bloomington, IN, 2011, p.166.
25. This quote has been attributed to John Calvin but may be a mish-mash of sound bites made by Irenaeus, Athanasius, and Augustine.
26. Anna Bartlett Warner, Hymn: "Jesus loves me," 1860, website: www.hymntime.com/tch/htm/j/e/s/jesuslme.htm (accessed March 10, 2014).
27. Joseph Prince, *Unmerited Favor: Your Supernatural Advantage for a Successful Life*, Joseph Prince Teaching Resources: Singapore, 2009, p.13.

PART B: 12 Myths about the Hyper-Grace Gospel

1. G3341 (*metanoia*), Thayer's Greek Lexicon, website: concordances.org/greek/3341.htm (accessed March 18, 2014).
2. Nee, *The Normal Christian Life*, p.132.
3. John Sheasby, *The Birthright*, Zondervan: Grand Rapids, MI, 2010, p.68.
4. G3670 (*homologeo*), Thayer's Greek Lexicon, website: concordances.org/greek/3670.htm (accessed March 14, 2014). For a good example of Biblical confession, consider Romans 10:9: "If you confess (i.e., agree) with your mouth that Jesus is Lord and believe in your heart that God raised Him from the dead, you will be saved" (ESV).
5. Steve McVey, *Grace Walk*, Harvest House: Eugene, OR, 1995, p.125.
6. Lucado, *Grace*, p.83.
7. Clark Whitten, *Pure Grace*, Destiny Image: Shippensburg, PA, 2012, p.95.
8. Andrew Farley, *The Naked Gospel*, Zondervan: Grand Rapids, MI, 2009, p.149.
9. G863 (*aphiēmi*), Thayer's Greek Lexicon, website: concordances.org/greek/863.htm (accessed March 14, 2014).
10. Hall, *Grace Works*, p.170.
11. For more on how Jesus changed His message after the cross, see Paul Ellis, *The Gospel in Ten Words*, KingsPress: Birkenhead, New Zealand, 2012, chapter 2.
12. Smith, *The Lost Secret of the New Covenant*, pp.174–5.
13. Manning, *The Ragamuffin Gospel*, p.181.
14. Farley, *The Naked Gospel*, p.147.
15. Prince, *The Power of Right Believing*, pp.309–10.
16. Whitten, *Pure Grace*, p.117.
17. Joseph Prince, *Destined to Reign: The Secret to Effortless Success, Wholeness and Victorious Living*, 22 Media: Singapore, 2007, pp.122–3.
18. Nee, *The Normal Christian Life*, p.158.

19. Prince, *Destined to Reign*, p.75.
20. Dunn, *The Happy Gospel*, p.129.
21. Ellis, *The Gospel in Twenty Questions*, p.79.
22. C. H. Spurgeon, "The Holy Ghost: The great Teacher," Sermon, Christian Classics Ethereal Library, 1855, website: www.ccel.org/ccel/spurgeon/sermons01.xlvii.html (accessed March 18, 2014).
23. D. Martyn Lloyd-Jones, *Romans: Exposition of Chapter 6 — The New Man*, Banner of Truth: Edinburgh, UK, 1972, pp.8–9.
24. Jefferson Bethke, *Jesus > Religion: Why He is So Much Better than Trying Harder, Doing More, and Being Good Enough*, Nelson Books: Nashville, TN, 2013, p.150.
25. White, *Revelation to Transformation*, pp.69–70.
26. Wayne Jacobsen, *He Loves Me: Learning to Live in the Father's Affection*, Windblown Media: Newbury Park, CA, 2007, p.88.
27. Prince, *The Power of Right Believing*, p.160.
28. See, for example, 1 Corinthians 1:2–3, 1 Thessalonians 5:5–6. We'll look at some more scriptures exhorting us to be holy in Part C.
29. Wommack, *Grace*, p.5.
30. Jacobsen, *He Loves Me*, p.23.
31. Darrin Hufford, *The Misunderstood God: The Lies Religion Tells About God*, Windblown Media: Newbury Park, CA, 2009, p.133.
32. This poem was attributed to John Bunyan (1628–1688) by Corrie Ten Boom in her "Personal Testimony," presented at "Let the Earth Hear His Voice: The International Congress on World Evangelization," Lausanne Switzerland, July 16–25, 1974, website: www.lausanne.org/docs/lau1docs/0279.pdf (accessed March 10, 2014).
33. Tchividjian, *One Way Love*, p.186.
34. That said, the grace of God has opened my eyes to the treasure in the Bible like never before. Some days I probably spend six or seven hours reading it. I don't think of this as "Bible study." It's what I do for fun.

PART C: A Response to Michael L. Brown

1. In the subtitle of his book, Dr. Brown conveys his concern that the modern grace message is "dangerous." How dangerous? He never says but he drops enough hints for you to realize that the hyper-grace gospel could be destructive to your faith. Directly or indirectly it may cause you to lose your salvation. Other opponents of the modern grace message are less reserved when warning of the dangers of the hyper-grace gospel. One of Dr. Brown's endorsers has said that we who preach it "will be held accountable for the spiritual death of millions." Source: Steve Hill, "The spiritual avalanche that could kill millions," *Charisma News*, December 11, 2012, website www.charismanews.com/opinion/34894-steve-hill-the-spiritual-avalanche-that-could-kill-millions (accessed March 25, 2014).

2. Michael L. Brown, *Hyper-Grace: Exposing the Dangers of the Modern Grace Message*, Charisma House: Lake Mary, FL, 2014.

3. Prince, *The Power of Right Believing*, pp.126–7.

4. Andrew Farley, *The Naked Gospel*, p.216.

5. Personal correspondence with the author.

6. Not every hyper-grace preacher will agree with me when I say the whole world was forgiven at the cross. The difference hinges on whether one defines forgiveness as a gift given or a gift received. I take my lead from John the Baptist who said Jesus took away "the sin of the world," and John the apostle who said Jesus is the propitiation for the sins "of the whole world" (John 1:29, 1 John 2:2, ESV). Both were referring to the finished work of the cross.

7. In a related note (see his endnote 11 on page 256), Dr. Brown repeats a comment he heard from a hyper-grace pastor that Jesus' words in the Revelation letters are too hard to understand. I beg to differ and would direct any interested reader to the archives of Escape to Reality (escapetoreality.org/index). There you can find many grace-based posts unpacking Christ's words to the churches in Ephesus, Laodicea, Sardis, etc.

8. Whitten, *Pure Grace*, p.91. Which other hyper-grace authors discuss 1 John 1:9? Joseph Prince discusses it in chapter 13 of *Unmerited Favor*; Andrew Wommack discusses it in chapter 4 of *The True Nature of God*; Jeremy White discusses it in chapter 8 of *The Gospel Uncut*; Andrew Farley discusses it in chapter 22 of *The Naked Gospel* and chapter 24 of *God Without Religion*; and I discuss it in chapter 2 of *The Gospel in Ten Words*.

9. For more on these distinctions, see my article, "Why confession is still good for you," Escape to Reality, October 25, 2012, website: wp.me/pNzdT-1rc (accessed March 10, 2014).

10. W. Ian Thomas, *If I Perish, I Perish: The Christian Life as Seen in the Book of Esther*. Torchbearer, Estes Park, CO, 1967/1993, p.47.

11. Ellis, *The Gospel in Twenty Questions*, p.119.

12. I owe this insight to Jennifer MacRae Howie who shared it with me after reading an earlier draft of this book.

13. C. H. Spurgeon, "All of Grace," Sermon, The Spurgeon Archive, date unknown, website: www.spurgeon.org/all_of_g.htm (accessed March 25, 2014).

14. Andrew Wommack, *A Better Way to Pray*, Andrew Wommack Ministries (Europe): Walsall, England, 2009, p.27. If you like this classic "Wommackism," you can find more in a post entitled, "Wommackisms – Top 20 Andrew Wommack quotes," Escape to Reality, July 11, 2011, website: wp.me/pNzdT-11c (accessed March 10, 2014).

15. See my article, "Three reasons why I don't preach repentance (turn from sin)," Escape to Reality, November 28, 2011, website: wp.me/pNzdT-19Y (accessed March 10, 2014).

16. G5048 (*teleioō*) Strong's Exhaustive Concordance, website: concordances.org/greek/5048.htm (accessed March 10, 2014). Jesus calls to imperfect, incomplete man and says, "Be perfect (*teleios* or complete), therefore, as your heavenly Father is perfect (complete)" (Matt. 5:48). Apart from Him you never will be, but in Him you are and always shall be.

17. Bill Gillham, *Lifetime Guarantee*, Harvest House: Eugene, OR, 1993, p.126.

18. Ralph Harris, *God's Astounding Opinion of You*, Harvest House: Eugene, OR, 2007, p.20.

19. Quote taken from "Lloyd-Jones on Holiness," CultureWatch, website: billmuehlenberg.com/2014/01/22/lloyd-jones-on-holiness (accessed March 20, 2014).

20. Bill Gillham, *Lifetime Guarantee*, pp.181–2.

21. Ibid., p.202.

22. See also Romans 8:15–16, 2 Corinthians 1:2, Galatians 4:6–7, and Ephesians 1:5 if you have any doubts about your adoption in Christ.

23. Since I don't have space to unpack 1 Corinthians 11 here, I direct the interested reader to chapters 10 and 13 of my book *The Gospel in Twenty Questions*.

24. G1381 (*dokimazo*), Strong's Exhaustive Concordance, website: concordances.org/greek/1381.htm (accessed March 14, 2014).

25. Dr. Brown argues that Revelation 3:1–2 destroys hyper-grace claims. I'm not sure how it does but if you are interested in a grace-based interpretation of Christ's words to the saints and sinners at Sardis, I encourage you to check out my post entitled "Incomplete deeds: The Zombie church of Sardis," Escape to Reality, April 11, 2010, website: wp.me/pNzdT-8h (accessed March 10, 2014). In a related note, Dr. Brown queries my view that many and possibly all of the Laodiceans were unsaved (see his endnote 23 on page 267). He argues that the Laodiceans must have been believers because the term used to describe them, *ekklesia*, always refers to churches or congregations of believers. This is both circular reasoning ("Paul Ellis always speaks the truth because Paul Ellis says so") and incorrect (alternative translations of *ekklesia* can be found in Acts 19:32, 39, 41). In my observation, most congregations contain a mix of believers and unbelievers.

26. Prince, *The Power of Right Believing*, pp.203–4.

27. Sheasby, *The Birthright*, p.102.

28. Paul Ellis, *The Gospel in Ten Words*, p.21.

29. For more on this, see my article, "What is the 'whole' gospel?" Escape to Reality, Dec. 6, 2012, website: wp.me/pNzdT-1tV (accessed March 10, 2014).

30. So how do grace preachers interpret Jesus' words about chopping off hands? For my take on these harsh words, see my article, "Chop off your hand?! Was Jesus serious?" Escape to Reality, April 7, 2011, website: wp.me/pNzdT-Hj (accessed March 10, 2014).

31. C. H. Spurgeon, "The barley field on fire," Sermon No.563, The Spurgeon Archive, date unknown, website: www.spurgeon.org/sermons/0563.htm (accessed February 18, 2014).

32. Andrew Wommack, *The True Nature of God*, Andrew Wommack Ministries (Europe): Walsall, England, 2008, p.2.

33. Ellis, *The Gospel in Twenty Questions*, pp.10–11.

34. Cornel Marais, *So You Think Your Mind is Renewed*, New Nature Publications, Hong Kong, 2009, p.8.

35. Andrew Farley, *God Without Religion*, Baker Books: Grand Rapids, MI, 2011, p.31.

36. Which is that honoring your parents is always a good idea. Whether you're under grace or law, it's a good thing to do. We are not righteous because we honor our parents; we honor our parents because we are righteous.

37. Steve McVey, *Grace Rules*, Harvest House: Eugene, OR, 1998, p.75.

38. If this makes no sense to you, I encourage you to check out my article, "How to walk after the flesh in 20 easy lessons," Escape to Reality, August 11, 2011, website: wp.me/pNzdT-135 (accessed March 10, 2014).

39. Joseph Prince, "How believers fall from grace," Sermon, April 17, 2011, website: youtu.be/h2c0SbFim6w (accessed March 10, 2014). For more on the different types of covenants I recommend a little book by Chad M. Mansbridge called *He Qualifies You* and a bigger book by Malcolm Smith called *The Lost Secret of the New Covenant*.

40. Farley, *The Naked Gospel*, p.80.

41. Ellis, *The Gospel in Ten Words*, p.92.

42. Brian Zahnd, *Beauty Will Save the World*, Charisma House: Lake Mary, FL, 2012, p.186.

43. See my article, "By which gospel are you saved? The gospel of grace!" Escape to Reality, April 11, 2010, website: wp.me/pNzdT-l7 (accessed March 10, 2014).

44. Steve McVey, *52 Lies Heard in Church Every Sunday*, Harvest House: Eugene Oregon, 2011, p.75.

45. Ellis, *The Gospel in Ten Words*, pp.117–8.

46. Derek Prince, "The divine exchange," Sermon, Escape to Reality, 1987, website: escapetoreality.files.wordpress.com/2010/06/the-divine-exchange.pdf (accessed March 10, 2014).

47. Andrew Wommack, "Living in the balance of grace and faith," Andrew Wommack Ministries, date unknown, website: www.awmi.net/extra/article/living_balance (accessed February 17, 2014).

48. Ellis, *The Gospel in Twenty Questions*, p.176.

49. Most hyper-grace preachers would be of the opinion that the fearsome warnings of Hebrews do not apply to believers. This is a view I have put forward in two posts: (1) "Hebrews 6:4–6," Escape to Reality, February 28, 2012, website: wp.me/pNzdT-1eb (accessed March 10, 2014), and (2)

"Hebrews 10:26," Escape to Reality, February 15, 2012, website: wp.me/pNzdT-1dW (accessed March 10, 2014).

Final Word
1. Whitten, *Pure Grace*, p.171.

Acknowledgements

This book came about by accident. After reading Michael L. Brown's *Hyper-Grace*, I thought I would jot down a few notes for Escape to Reality readers. I showed my notes to some friends and they suggested I add something up front that could be used as a stand-alone introduction to the hyper-grace gospel. "Give us a hyper-grace handbook," said one. So I wrote what became Parts A and B of the book you're now reading, and my response to Dr. Brown became Part C.

I am grateful to Dr. Brown for providing the spark that lit the fire and my friends who shaped the content and tone of the finished product. I would particularly like to acknowledge the constructive feedback and assistance provided by Chad M. Mansbridge, Steve Hackman, Tony Ide, and Presley Watson. I also want to thank E2R readers who acted as a sounding board for many of the thoughts found in this book.

For their assistance in proofreading the book I am grateful to Judy Fake, Caroline Passier, and Jennifer MacRae Howie.

Again, my deepest appreciation goes to my hyper-gracious wife Camilla who helped me in more ways than I can describe.

The good news may be the best news you never heard!

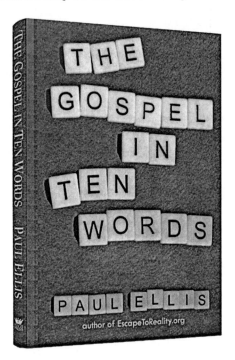

At a time when many are hearing mixed messages about the love of God, *The Gospel in Ten Words* is a welcome reminder of the good news revealed by Jesus.

This book will take you to the heavenly treasure rooms of grace and leave you awestruck at the stunning goodness of God.

You will discover the secret to walking in divine favor and experiencing freedom in every aspect of your life. You will learn who you really are and why you were born.

Best of all, you will come face to face with the One who has called you to the thrilling adventure of living loved.

AVAILABLE NOW!

Amazon, BAM!, Barnes & Noble, Book Depository, and other good retailers!

A good question can change your life!

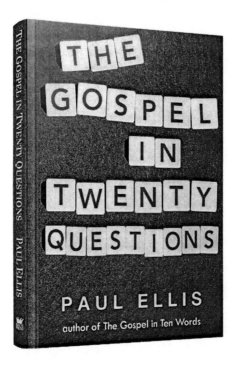

Questions are keys to treasure. They are stepping stones to revelation and doorways to discovery.

What is God like? What does He want from me? Should I do everything Jesus said? How does God deal with me when I sin? How do I reconcile contradictory scriptures? Does God make us sick to teach us things? What is the unforgiveable sin? What are heavenly rewards? And many more!

The questions in this book will take you places. They will cause you to dance on the uplands of your Father's favor. Best of all, they will lead you to a deeper relationship with Jesus, who is the greatest Answer of all.

AVAILABLE NOW!

Amazon, BAM!, Barnes & Noble, Book Depository, and other good retailers!

Escape to Reality – The Greatest Hits!

Grace Disco: Greatest Hits, Vol. 1
Is God's love unconditional? / God is good, but how good is he? / Son, servant or friend of God? / How well did I understand grace before I understood grace? / The top twelve blessings in the new covenant / The cure for guilt / What is holiness? / Does God use correction fluid? / Take up your cross daily / Faith is a rest / *and much more!*

Grace Classics: Greatest Hits, Vol. 2
By which gospel are you saved? / Are you religious? / Does God give and take away? / Seven signs you're under law / When doing good is bad for you / How to walk after the flesh in twenty lessons / Where was God in the Connecticut school shooting? / What happens to Christians who commit suicide? / *and much more!*

Grace Party: Greatest Hits, Vol. 3
The gospel in one word, two words... / God believes in you! / Are you hot enough for God? / Ten myths about the Holy Spirit / Healthy vs unhealthy confession / What was Last Adam's greater work? / Can unbelievers take communion / Building ramps for the mentally ill / *and much more!*

AVAILABLE NOW!

Amazon, BAM!, Barnes & Noble, Book Depository, Booktopia, Eden.co.uk,
Kinokuniya, Loot.co.za, Nile.com.au, Waterstones,
W.H. Smith, and other good retailers.